The Quinnipiack Indians and Their Reservation

THE QUINNIPIACK INDIANS AND THEIR RESERVATION

BY

CHARLES HERVEY TOWNSHEND

Of "Raynham"

NEW HAVEN, CONN., U. S. A.

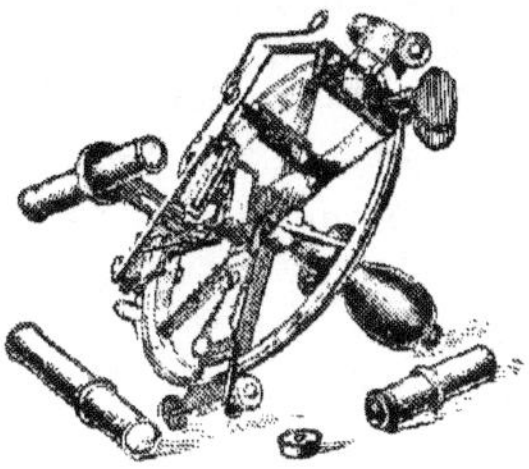

PRESS OF TUTTLE, MOREHOUSE & TAYLOR, NEW HAVEN, CONN.

PREFACE.

In presenting this illustrated volume the author takes this opportunity to mention that it has been prepared by request from a paper read before the New Haven Colony Historical Society and now appears in Vol VI of the papers published by that organization

About the year 1870 it occurred to him that during his boyhood days he had often seen framentary evidences of the occupation of New Haven region by the Quinnipiac Indians, in the shape of implements of war and the chase, found on their reservation, on which he was born. There were also heads of arrows and tomahawks remaining in his family keeping, and, with these as a basis, a collection was at once commenced Assisted by old schoolmates and neighbors, enough objects were gathered to make an exhibit which later has been reproduced by the Photogravure Process, giving thereon credit to those of my friends who were so kind as to present me with some of their findings

While making this collection, a desire was stimulated to know more of the Quinnipiacks and searches have brought to light a mass of most interesting material which has been abstracted from the records and used in the compilation of a more extended work With these surface gleamings many fragments have been saved with the hope to interest and to point out to others who are more gifted with the pen a fruitful field of inquiry, should they be induced to prepare from the same records a more perfect history of "the Quinnipiack Indians and Their Reservation."

Besides the Colonial Records, history and traditions, original papers in the possession of private persons have been examined, and in addition other accounts given me verbally by old residents, whose association with early days would impart an additional value to what they could communicate orally, have been carefully noted down for comparison with documentary evidence, which comparison has shown a surprising agreement between the two

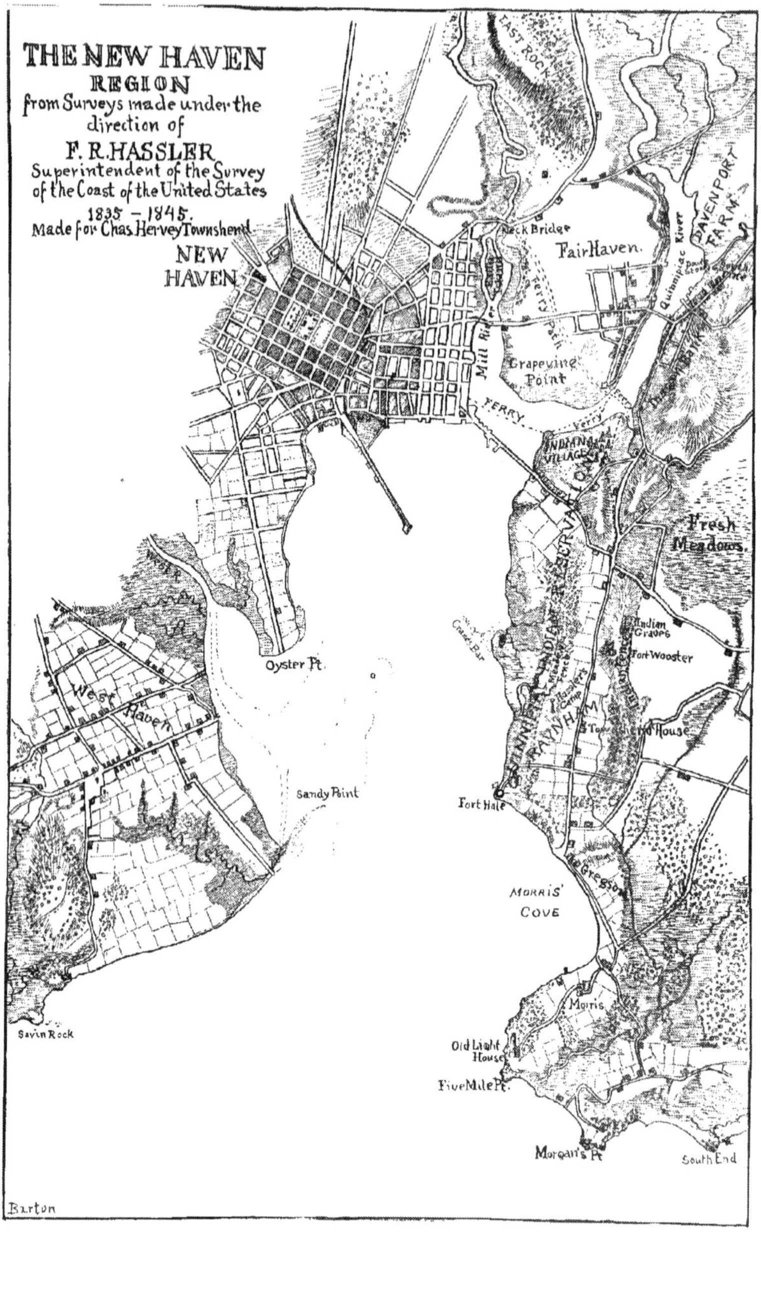
THE NEW HAVEN
REGION
from Surveys made under the
direction of
F. R. HASSLER
Superintendent of the Survey
of the Coast of the United States
1835 – 1845.
Made for Chas. Hervey Townshend.
NEW HAVEN
EAST ROCK
Neck Bridge
Fair Haven.
Quinnipiac River
DAVENPORT FARM
Mill River
Ferry Path
Grapevine Point
FERRY
Ferry
INDIAN VILLAGE
Fresh Meadows.
Indian Graves
Fort Wooster
Townshend House
Fort Hale
Oyster Pt.
West Haven
Sandy Point
MORRIS' COVE
Morris
Old Light House
Five Mile Pt.
Morgan's Pt.
South End
Savin Rock
Barton

THE QUINNIPIACK INDIANS AND THEIR RESERVATION

BY

CHARLES HERVEY TOWNSHEND

Of "Raynham," New Haven, Conn , U S A

THE Quinnipiack Indians were a small and somewhat scattered tribe speaking the Algonquin language and found by Europeans in actual possession of this beautiful region which still bears their name. These Indians with their neighbors, the Pequots and Mohegans, were probably first mentioned by the Florentine navigator, Verrazano, who, in the employ of Francis I of France, in search of a passage to Cathay, examined this coast in 1524 Later mention of them is made by the Dutch explorer, Adrian Block, who made a chart of Long Island Sound, in the early part of the year 1614 naming the country "Rodenbergh "

The learned J Hammond Trumbull thus speaks of their territory·

"Quinnipiac—Quillipiac, originally the land near the head of New Haven Harbor, and the estuary of the Quinnipiac and Mill rivers

"The name 'Quinni-pe-auke' means 'long water-land' or country It is the equivalent of Kennebec (Abn) Kooenbeki

"In both the Mohegan and Narragansett dialects the first syllable was pronounced 'quin', by the Connecticut River Indians 'quil', and by the Indians west of the long water, 'quin', hence the variety of forms under which the name appears in early records "

The Dutch called the natives of this region "Quirepeys " President Stiles, of Yale College, heard the name from an East Haven Indian as "Quinnepyooghq ' Lieut Richard Davenport, in a letter to Gov Winthrop of Massachusetts

Bay, dated "Possession House, [Pequot] (New London Harbor) this 4th of ye 5th (July) month, 1637, O S," writes "but I must extole Quenepiake" Captain John Underhill—"That famous place called Queenapiok which rather exceeds the former (Saybrook) in goodness It hath a fair river fit for the harbouring of ships and abounds with rich and goodly meadows This [Quinnipiack] lyes thirty miles from the upper Plantations on the river Connecticut"

Major John Mason, the conqueror of the Pequot Indians at Mystic Fort, May, 1637, in his brief history of this war, writes the name "Quinnypiog' He informs us in his history, of the causes which led to the exploration and final settlement by the English here He says "About a fortnight after our return home (to Hartford) which was about one month after the fight at Mystick, there arrived in Pequot River several vessels from Massachusetts, Captain Israel Stoughton being Commander in Chief, and with him about 120 men, sent by the Colony to pursue the war against the Pequots The enemy had all fled before they came, except some few stragglers who were surprised by the Mohegans and other Indians, and by them delivered to the Massachusetts soldiers Connecticut Colony being informed thereof, sent forth forty men, Captain Mason (the writer) being Commander in Chief, together with some other gentlemen, to meet those from Massachusetts in Pequot Harbor After some time in consultation they concluded to join together and pursue the Pequots who had fled westward toward Manhattan, and so forthwith the forces marched after them, discovering several places where the Pequots had rendezvoused and lodged, the foe making but little haste by reason of their children and want of provisions, being forced to dig for clams and to procure such other sustenance as the wilderness afforded, our vessels in the meantime sailing along the shore in close company At Guilford the Pequots were overtaken and one of their chiefs while making his escape by swimming across a small harbor, was shot to death with arrows by the friendly Indians, whose head they cut off and placed it in the crotch of a tree which in time grew around the skull and the place took the name of Sachems Head '

"In about the space of three days we arrived at New Haven Harbor, then called 'Quinnypiog,' and seeing a great smoak in the woods not far distant, and supposing that some of the Pequots, our enemies, might be there, we hastened ashore; but quickly discovered them to be Connecticut Indians, then we returned aboard our vessels, where we stayed some short time, having sent a Pequot captive upon discovery, whom we named 'Luz' and of whom mention will be made hereafter"

The numerous modes of spelling this unique Indian name Quinnipiack seem to have crystallized into Quinnipiack soon after the arrival of the Governor Eaton settlers This is shown in the Rev John Davenport's letter, (on file in the British Museum,) to the Lady Mary Vere, which announced the arrival of Fenwick's ship, the "St John" of London, Captain Richard Russell, with the Rev Henry Whitefield's Guilford settlers This letter was written at Quinnipiack ye 26th of ye 7th month, [September] 1639, O S Mr Davenport in describing Quinnipiack's attractions says "The sight of the Harbor did so please the Captain of the ship that he called it the 'Fair Haven'"

In Governor Eaton's letter "To the much honored Governor, Deputy Governor and Assistants of the Colony of Massachusetts Bay," dated the 12th day of the 1st month, [March] 1638, announcing the intention of his company to remove thence to Quinnipiack which he had explored and held by right of prior occupation, with a party of eight men in the autumn previous, and domiciled in a hut on the bank of West Creek, he says "We hope in mercy, and have sent letters to Connecticut for a speedy transacting of the purchase of the parts about Quillypiack from the natives which *may pretend title thereunto*, by which act we are absolutely irrevocably engaged that way"

These early allusions to the Indian name I have collated for purposes of comparison with the name in the recorded Treaty, spelled *Quinopiocke*, which seems at the time to have been accepted as correct

The late Dr Leonard Bacon, who gave the name much thought and study, an authority which I accept, decided this matter when the inscription was graven on the Founder's slab, set over the door of our historic First Church edifice, and so let the name stand "Quinnipiack"

A repetition of early Colonial and Indian history will only be indulged in when necessary to connect fragmentary evidence still extant regarding the opening of the Quinnipiack region for settlement, and in giving in abridged outline a combination of the facts and circumstances which led to the Pequot War, which occurred in the early summer of 1637, and forced the English Colonies of Massachusetts and Connecticut into a struggle for self-preservation *

These Pequots, near neighbors of the Quinnipiacks, whose last chief, Sassacus, was said to have been killed soon after the Fairfield or Sosco Swamp fight, June 1637, were a warlike tribe, which Indian historians tell us sprang from a remnant of the more powerful Taratines, who in early times inhabited the northern part of Norembuigha and were known by the Norman and Biscayan fishing voyagers who annually visited this coast † They had brought under their sway the more southwestern tribes which inhabited the section of what was then known to the English as North Virginia, bordering on the shores of Long Island Sound, and occupying their lands by the right of conquest, holding autocratic sway over the neighboring tribes, and collecting, when disposed, extortionate tribute from these vassals, as Governor Eaton's treaties with the Quinnipiacks abundantly show

The Quinnipiacks were the next tribe adjoining the Niantics and Pequots on their western range and occupied lands which were claimed also by the powerful Mohawk tribe, living westward of the newly discovered river of Hendrick Hudson and to whom they were also compelled to pay tribute The Quin-

* The Connecticut Colony declared war against the Pequot Indians May 1st, 1637

† "The Puritans in Holland, England and America,' Vol I, p 388

"While France sent annually (Temp Elizabeth) 500 vessels to New Foundland fishing banks even the home fisheries around the English coast fell into the hands of foreigners"

"When Sir Humphrey Gilbert went to New Foundland in 1583 and took possession of the country in the name of Elizabeth, as an unknown land, he found there 36 vessels of other nations engaged in catching fish" nipiacks were frequently distressed by marauding bands from both the Pequots and Mohawks, and were at the time we speak of reduced by a plague which had scourged their country and nearly driven them out of existence, making it necessary for them to seek protection, which they willingly did, from the English. The Quinnipiacks, at the date of the Eaton treaty, had been reduced to forty-six fighting men and including squaws and papooses numbering in the neighborhood of about one hundred and fifty persons

Signs of the trails followed at this period by the tribute collectors, whether Pequot or Mohawk, through the Quinnipiack region, are still extant at Milford, at what is now the site of a picturesque bridge built by that town to commemorate its settlement; and at the West River at Westville, through Hamilton Park to the plateau which faces the harbor between Union and East streets and which in Colonial times was called the Oyster Shell Fields, thence northward crossing Mill River over the rocky ledge at Whitneyville, and turning southward under East Rock, across the neck to the East River, which was forded during low tides at Fair Haven ("Dragon"), thence to the principal village* of the Quinnipiacks, where distinct signs of this trail are still to be seen on the east side of the ridge southward from the Quinnipiack bridge to about Four Corners, and then forking, one branch to Stony river and the other to Solitary Cove Here, near springs of cold soft, clear water (the cold spring) lies a deposit of sea shells several feet deep, and imbedded therein have been found implements of

* The site of the principal village of the Quinnipiack Indians at the time Governor Eaton's settlers landed was on the elevation south of the Quinnipiack bridge and bounded by Farren and Fairmount avenues so far south as Fulton street and crossed in the center by Lancraft street

The country being heavily wooded, it is probable that vistas were made by the Indians looking southward on the meadows and harbor and northward on the Quinnipiack river and meadows, with East Rock and Mount Carmel range in full view

In the depression on the east side of this village, now as then, ran a brooklet [giving water supply to the Indians] across Ferry and South Quinnipiack streets into the river from the cold spring located in the rear of Captain George E Lancraft's house This spring is in the line which formerly divided the Tuttle and Pardee lands east of the Ferry farm, which they bought of the town war, the chase, and the field, with kitchen utensils Many of these, which are among the intensely interesting specimens at hand [exhibited], were gathered and presented to the writer by the Hon Asa Fabrique, Capt George Edwin Lancraft, George Hitchcock, Esq, and George H Townsend, Esq, whose residences are in the Indian fields and whom the writer again thanks for enriching his own growing archaeological collection

But we must not linger here in this charming spot surrounded with vistas landward and seaward, but will continue the Indian trail southeastward through the old and new Indian fields to the Solitary (or Morris) Cove, under Tuttle (or Reservoir) Hill, passing the Fresh Meadows ("Great Swamp") eastward, once the powwow* place of the Quinnipiacks, where Indian tradition tells us many sacrifices were made to their gods Here in this locality has been seen by returning citizens of East Haven, during late hours at night, jack-o-lanterns,† giving a hideous aspect to this place where in the long distant past the powwows performed on the blackest nights, by the light of lurid camp fires, their hellish conjurations

* "Indian Sickness—how the Powows officiate —Roger Williams says 'When sick the priest came close to the sick person and perform many strange actions about him, and threatened and conjure out the sickness The poor people commonly die under their hands for alas, they administer nothing, but howl and war and hollow over them and begin the songs to the rest of the people who all join like a choir in prayer to their God for them '

Wood says 'The Powow sitting, the rest give attentive audience to his imprecations and invocations, and after the violent expressions of many a hideous bellowing and groaning he makes a stop and then all the auditors with one voice utter a short Canto, which done the powow still proceeds, sometimes roaring like a bear, other times groaning like a dying horse, foaming at the mouth like a chafed boar, smiting his naked breast and thighs with such violence as if mad, thus he will continue sometimes half a day '"

† This is what East Haven people call the 'Ghost," over the Peat Meadows "Will-o-the-wisp" or a "jack-o-lantern' A meteoric clammy vapor in the air which reflects light in the dark, commonly haunting church yards, fens and steaming out of a fat soil.

It also flies about rivers, hedges, etc, where there is a continual flux of air, and lead those imprudently following it, quite out of their way —*N E Gen and Hist Reg*, Vol II, p 75

Southward of the powwow place, on the northeast part of the hill and east of the trail to the Solitary Cove, was the burying place of the Quinnipiacks, and on the summit of the hill was their Palisade Fort, the site of which has been lately imparked (Fort Wooster Park) * Here is also the site of the ruins of Fort Wooster This fort was built during the last war with England and named in honor of the Connecticut martyr soldier and sailor Maj -Gen David Wooster (Yale College, class 1738) Here on this spot are the ancient Revolutionary (and War of 1812) earthworks which were occupied by the British General Tryon as his headquarters during the New Haven invasion, July 1779, but not till after a spirited defence by the patriots This was the Quinnipiack's "lookout" and signal-fire place, whence they invited traders from vessels in the Sound to our harbor to traffic for skins Here also on this very hill were lighted the signal fires which shone forth, directing the vessels that conveyed the pursuers of the Pequots to Quinnipiaek Harbor, and here in our harbor the miniature fleet sought shelter behind Sandy Point beach in the quiet roadstead off Oyster (City) Point until the return of the before mentioned spies ("Luz" and his two Quinnipiacks), who had been sent westward and who, on their return, reported that

* A bronze tablet set into a boulder on the north rampart of Fort Wooster was dedicated by the "Sons of Colonial Wars," followed with an oration by United States Senator Orville H Platt, July 5, 1895

"ON THIS SPOT A SIGNAL BEACON
WAS ESTABLISHED IN 1775
AND ABOUT THIS HILL
AMERICAN PATRIOTS
BRAVELY RESISTED A LARGE FORCE
OF INVADING BRITISH TROOPS
JULY 5, 1779
* * * * * * * * * * * *
TO HONOR THE DEEDS OF THE FATHERS
THE CONNECTICUT SOCIETY
SONS OF THE AMERICAN REVOLUTION
PLACED THIS TABLET 1895"

The procession to the hill was escorted by the 2d Company of Governor's Foot Guards of the State of Connecticut A grape shot found on the hill was presented by Park Commissioner the Hon James M Townsend, adding historic interest to the occasion the retiring Pequots had made a stand on an island in Sosco (Fairfield) Swamp * And on this hill during the Revolution

* This island, now overgrown with evergreen we are told, is in a swamp crossed by the New York and New Haven R R on its southern edge, and now reclaimed, wherein is still to be seen a pretty evergreen mount upon which the Pequots made their last stand in full view of Long Island Sound, and about half a mile east of the Saugatuck River

Hubbard, Indian Wars [Pequot War 1637] Copied from the Brayton Ives Collection 1891

P 28 "Our soldiers by God s assistance who were to make a final destruction of them were sent to persue them whatsoever way they should think best to make Our soldiers went by water to New Haven whethersoever there after arrival they were informed of a great number of them who had betaken themselves to a neighborhood place not far off whither they might hope it was not likely they should be pursued , but upon search they (the soldiers) found 50 or 60 Wigwams without Indians in any of them but they heard they had passed towards the Dutch Plantation, whereupon our soldiers that were there before, all embarked from Quillipiac and being landed there, they had not far to go to march into the place where it was thought probably they should either find or hear of them "

P 29 "They found sundry of them whom they slew or took prisoners, among whom were two (2) Sachems who they beheaded, and a third whether a king or a Sachem they gave him life if he would go and enquire where Sassacus was

He was told to be gone three (3) days but was gone eight (8), and was suspected (by the Pequots) of being a spy when he left They put to follow him to New Haven (Quinnipiac) harbour, and finding an old canoe on the shore lately cast adrift they paddled out into the bay, and were discovered by some one on the vessels which attended the soldiers by whom when taken up he made known what he had discovered

After he had left the Pequots on his return Sassacus the reigning Cheif, supposing him to have been a spy made his escape to the Mohawks, with about 80 of his tribe, and was by them murdered Providence guided our soldier at last On July 13th 1637, they lighted upon a great number of them at a small Indian town situated by the side of a swamp near the place where Fairfield or Stratfield now stands The native Indians of the place who had led them into the swamp on an island, came out and delivered themselves up, but the Peqouts stayed, and were here destroyed The swamp was surround by the soldiers standing 12 feet apart "

In the fight at "Sosco Swamp" were Mr Ludlow, Capt Mason, Mr Turner, Capt Patrick, Capt Trask, Lieut Davemport wounded in the belly with an arrow, Tho Sherman, Thomas Stanton an exact interperter

Mass Col Hist Soc , Vol IX, Fifth Series Trumbull Papers, 1885 ed , page 1 and 1812 war beacon signals were located, as the following notice from the "Connecticut Journal" and a sketch still extant bearing the signature of N Jocelin, Sc, N H, 1814, testifies The latter was found among the papers of the late

Richard Davenport to Gov Winthrop of Mass [1]

"To the Right Wortherly Honored Governor of Massachusetts these present Possession House[2] this 4th day of the week (month 6th 1637) Honored Sir—My most humble and due respect to your worship

Mi Deputy My Colonel with all the rest of oui noble workers

Sir The messengei staying foi us I must make haste How God hath dwelt with us, I doubt not but youi worship hath full intelligence by them fiom Block Island Now, since then departure there came some Mohigens to the house, and brought the (new)s of a great Sachem as they said greater than Sasacus he being Momonohuk's son—a mighty fellow of couiage, and one that I know by some experience his despeiateness in the swamp, foi, as I gathei by the discription of him and also the Indian's report that slew him, that he said that he killed one in the swamp shooting him in the belly and another he killed with arrows which was myself But blessed be God we all live Two days after this, the same Indian killed anothei who was then run away from Sasacus He said he thought that Sasacus was killed, foi that Momonohuk had beset the wigwams where they were and so fell upon them and the men lying at the dooi ian away But what credit to give it we know not Two days since I went up to the head of the rivei with twenty (20) men to cut corn and gather beanes, and coming thithei I found a great company of Mohegens who were returned to their country, about 500 of men, women, and children They were somewhat feaiful at first, but after spoke with us and lovingly entertained us, they tell for certain that Sassacus is killed so the formei suspected and forty men with him and some women Six men weie escaped whereof Momonohuk is one I perceive the Indians would be glad to make women of all the Pecotts now except the Sachems, Captains and Musketers, but them they would kill

They seem to feai Narrogansick men but hope the English will not suffei them to be wronged Captain Stoughton is gone a week since to

[1] This lettei was written from New London in August, 1637, neai the close of the Pequot War Some parts of it are illegible and particulaily the latter portion of it, but the name Richard Davemport as the writer is sufficiently cleai It is well known that he was on service as a Lieutenant in the Massachusetts Company and was wounded in the swamp fight as the wiitei of the letter says that he was

[2] 'The Possession House" was the house built by Stoughton on or neai the neck of land on which Fort Trumbull now stands in New London See Caulkins' History of New London, p 36 37 and note, also p 104–5 It is repeatedly mentioned in the discussion before the Commissioners of the United Colonies, of the Massachusetts title to the Pequot Country by conquest and occupation J Hammond Trumbull, Mass Col. Hist. Soc, lettei Mar. 1, 1884.

Dr Totton, and becoming the property of the late Thomas R Trowbridge, Esq, who kindly permitted the writer to reproduce this sketch for future publication

"The town of New Haven having this day erected a Beacon on Indian Hill at East Haven, now Beacon Hill, about a mile and a half southeast of the town, and ordered us, their Committee, to give public notice thereof, we now inform the public in general and the neighboring towns in particular, that the Beacon will be fired on Monday evening next, the 20th instant, at 6 o'clock, all persons are then desired to look out for the Beacon and take the bearings of it from their respective places of abode, that they may know where to look for it in case of an alarm, which will be announced by the firing of three Cannon If our enemy should attack us and we be under necessity of making use of this method to call in the assistance of our brethren, we request that all persons who come into the town will take care to be well armed with a good musket, bayonet and cartridge box well filled with cartridges, under their proper officer, and repair to the State House, where he will receive orders from Col Fitch what post to take

"The ministers of the several parishes of this and the neighboring towns are requested to mention to their respective congregations the time when the Beacon will be fired"

Phineas Bradley, Isaac Doolittle, James Rice, } *Commissioners*

New Haven, 14th November, 1775

Connecticut Plantation and I hear that the Sachems of Long Island do not wait for him with their tribute at the rivers mouth I suppose under favor this place will not prove good for a Plantation so far as I can judge having seen the greater part of the country but I must extol Quinepiacke and Marriadge Point [1]

But this I know you heard of I see not what business here will be for many men long I know not Capt Stoughton's mind till his return about marching (illegible) (the Nipnets home)? My Captain and myself are for it

(Some) of our soldiers have no mind to work, and how they could fight I know not They murmur much for butter and cheese etc, etc But I hope God will give so much wisdom to endeavor them pacifying I confess some spirits here will trouble a patient man My Captain humbly salutes you with the council For myself Dear Sir, I bless God that I am fully recovered of my hurt only some (illegible) I want, My Captain desires some goose shot by the first (rest of the letter illegible)

Indorsed Recd 6 th 25 day 1637 Richard Davenport

---

[1] 'Marriadge Point may have been Charles Island, off Milford, Conn, which is connected with the main land at low tide by a sand and cobble ridge formed by the action of the east and west tides, which at high water meet or, in sea parlance 'marry,' hence the name 'Marriadge Point' It may have been Stratford Point, which is an island made by a creek running from Housatonic River to Bridgeport Harbor' C H T

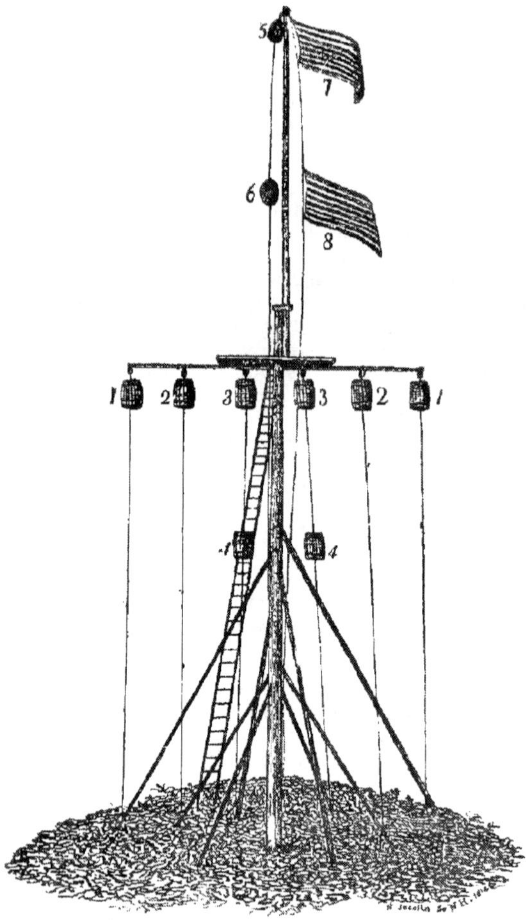

Explanation of the Telegraphic Signals on Beacon Hill, East Haven.

No. 1, N. E. arm, 1 Ship to Eastward.
No. 2, N. E. arm, 2 Ships to Eastward.
No. 3, N. E. arm, 3 Ships to Eastward.
No. 1 & 3, N. E. arm, 4 Ships to Eastward.
No. 1, N. E. arm, Halfmast, Fleet to Eastward.
No. 5, Topmast Head, Brig to Eastward.
No. 5 & 6, Topmast Head, 2 Brigs to Eastward.
No. 6, Half Topmast, 1 Schooner to Eastward.
No. 5 & 6, Half Topmast, 2 Schooners to Eastward.
No. 4, N. E. arm, Halfmast, 1 or more Sloops to Eastward.
No. 2, N. E. arm, Halfmast, Barges to Eastward.

No. 1, S. W. arm, 1 Ship to Westward.
No. 2, S. W. arm, 2 Ships to Westward.
No. 3, S. W. arm, 3 Ships to Westward.
No. 1 & 3, S. W. arm, 4 Ships to Westward.
No. 1, S. W. arm, Halfmast, Fleet to Westward.
No. 7, Topmast Head, Brig to Westward.
No. 7 & 8, Topmast Head, 2 Brigs to Westward.
No. 8, Half Topmast, 1 Schooner to Westward.
No. 7 & 8, Half Topmast, 2 Schooners to Westward.
No. 4, S. W. arm, Halfmast, Sloop to Westward.
No. 2, S. W. arm, Halfmast, Barges to Westward.

There was a signal master's watch house in fort.

When the Fort Wooster beacon was discontinued a circular, cage-shaped cap which allowed less resistance to the elements, and made of sheet iron or tin, was mounted on a pole twenty feet above, and just west of the powder magazines within the ruins of the fort. It was used by survey parties, and as a sea mark, to guide light draft vessels from the westward over the shoals off Savin Rock into the harbor channel, the range being the beacon brought to bear over the red brick arched gateway of Fort Hale.

Near this spot now is a U. S. Coast Survey triangulation stone, copper tipped, to mark the exact site.

On receipt of the information thus given the miniature army of pursuers, under the brave Mason of Connecticut, and Stoughton and Turner of Massachusetts, disembarked, leaving their vessels guarded in the quiet harbor of Quinnipiack, and accompanied by Higginson, the interpreter, and Uncas, chief of the Mohegans, and their Indian allies, followed the lead of these spies to the successful and final issue of the campaign. The object of the expedition accomplished in the complete annihilation of the bloodthirsty Pequots, and the victory won, the triumphant band returned to Quinnipiack, taking with them many captives, whose final tragic fate history recites with a shudder, which leaves a stain which can never be erased from the pages of Colonial history.

The expedition here rested for a few days, during which respite (in early June) the natural beauty and advantages of this region were examined. The party then returned homeward to Boston and Hartford with the glad tidings concerning this promised land, the Massachusetts contingent arriving at Boston just about the time of the landing of the Eaton company from the ship "Hector," Captain Fernes, from London, June 26th, 1637. This Eaton company had sailed from London early in the month of April previous, and, while undecided where to settle, were induced to a final settlement here (Quinnipiack) by Captain Turner, of Lynn, afterwards the Miles Standish of New Haven Colony.* (He was lost in the celebrated Phan-

* Whitman's Ancient and Honorable Artillery Company, Boston, 2d ed., p. 54-5. Capt. Nathenial Turner, 12th on the Roll and Charter Member; he lived in Nahant St., Lynn. Requested to be made Freeman Oct.

tom Ship) The Eaton party sailed from Boston March 30th, 1638, in open boats, coming via a water passage through Cape Cod and arrived at Quinnipiack about April 15th, following *

19, 1630 Took oath July 3, 1632, and in Boston and Lynn has the prefix of respect Mr Rep the 1st seven (7) sessions of the General Court and member of the first Quarterly Court at Salem, 1636 [1]

In 1633 Captain of the Militia in Lynn —In 1637 he had command in several expeditions against the Pequot Indians, and was a Captain in the Stoughton expedition when he acquired a desire for New Haven

In 1638 he sold his land on Sagamore Hill to Mr Edward Holyoke, and removed to Quillipiacke where he with others began a new settlement called New Haven

In 1639 he was one of the seven (7) members of the first church in that place In 1640 he purchased for the town, of Ponus an Indian Sagamore the tract of land which is now the town of Stamford, for which he paid in coats, hoes, and hatchets —(See Hall's History of Norwalk , also Hubbard's Indian Wars See also Cotton Mather)

His active and enterprising life was soon after terminated in a melancholy manner In Jan 1646, he sailed from New Haven for England (the ship was hauled down through a canal cut through the ice to Long Island Sound) with Capt Lamberton in a vessel which was never heard of more.

In Jan 1648 it is said that the apparition of a ship was seen under full sail moving up the harbour of New Haven a little before sunset on a pleasant afternoon and that as it approached the shore it slowly vanished —(See the Rev Mr Pierpoint s letter)[2]

The following epitaph was written to Capt Turner's memory

"Deep in the Atlantic cove his body sleeps,
Where the dark sea his ceaseless motion keeps
While the Phantom Ships are wrecked along the shore
To warn his friend that he will come no more,
But he, who governs all with impulse free,
Can bring from Basham and the deepest sea
And when he calls our Turner must return
Though now his ashes fill no sacred urn "[3]

* The following Sunday, April 18, Rev John Davenport preached to the settlers under the famous oak tree, corner College and George streets

[1] His house in Saugus took fire from an oven about midnight 10 1-1636, and burned to the ground with all in it save the family

[2] This was perhaps from a mirage frequently seen from the town and "Raynham " side of the harbour A ship may have been on the south side of Long Island and its reflected image taken for Lamberton's ship I have witnessed Long Island Sound mirages in my boyhood days — C H T.

[3] Longfellow, Phantom Ship of New Haven

On the east side of Beacon Hill ran the Indian fence which marks the reservation by a bush fence on the east extending southward It began on the south side of the country road east of Four Corners, and ran southward towards Mr Gregson's farm, a tract at Solitary Cove of one hundred and thirty-three acres of second division land, granted him August 5th, 1644 On the west side of this hill along the salt marsh was the meadow fence, a remnant of which also remains, and as the boundaries of the old and new Indian fields may interest—this being the first reservation to any tribe of natives in this country that we have any record of, it seems entirely fit to give them here, viz "From the old Ferry Point at Red Rock, Quinnipiac Bridge, to the Solitary Cove (Black Rock) on the west On the north the road or the Indian trail now closed, from the Pardee Ferry to Stoney River On the east, from the said road southward along the foot of Grave or Beacon Hill (east side) and the road that runs from Bridge Swamp to the Solitary Cove The Black Rock mentioned is on the southwest bounds of this reservation and is of basaltic formation It was formerly a prominent object, standing in bold relief on the northern horn of the crescent-shaped Morris (Solitary) Cove It was first sought for defensive purposes, as the records show, by order of the Colonial Court, February 20, 1657, brothers Andrews and Munson being empowered as commissioners to treat with the Indians to exchange lands therefor, and on February 26th, 1660, "at an adjourned Town meeting the Governor asked that it might be Considered the Settling of a Village near ye Black Rock and something be thought of our defense, for the furtherance of which brothers Andrews and Munson were desired to treat with ye Indians about exchange of lands" Here stood old Fort Hale, named for another Connecticut martyr, Captain Nathan Hale, who was also a graduate of Yale College (class 1773) The new fort, now in ruins, was built during the late war of the Rebellion, on the site of a former Fort Hale, which was constructed during the second war with England, 1812–14 The latter fort occupied the site of the Black Rock Fort of the American Revolution, which was built in 1776 The works of this Revolutionary fort were manned by a detachment of matrosses, nineteen men, with three field pieces, under the command of Lieutenant Bishop, who, on the morning of July 5th, 1779, opened fire on both divisions of the British while, under the command of Maj.-Gens Tryon and Garth, making a landing in boats from a fleet of forty-nine sail commanded by Sir George Collier, Kt., and with such undaunted spirit and bravery were their guns served that the town was not made an easy capture

Concerning this Black Rock Fort, now still known as Fort Hale, and its neighbor, also in ruins, on Beacon Hill (Fort Wooster), and regarding the battle fought July 5th, 1779 at "Raynham" by the Patriots with the second division of the British invaders under Major General Tryon, in which engagement many of the enemy were slain, an extended history has been written, and will some day be published

The Indian Reservation of which I write covered an area of about twelve hundred acres The Quinnipiacks were reserved by the colonists This tract is on the east side toward the river Connecticut This is shown by the two recorded deeds or treaties still extant, made at the time when the Indians sold to Governor Eaton and his company of English Planters all their *pretended right* to their country, a territory more than 10 miles square, extending inland from Long Island Sound, and embracing both sides of New Haven harbor and the river which still bears their name *

On this reservation, these Indians were allowed by deeds or treaties made November 24th, 1638 (a verbatim copy from the New Haven Town Records is here appended which was recorded by the hand of Secretary Gibbard) the right to hunt, fish and cut wood for their necessary wants, and if affrighted

* Goodwin's Pilgrim Republic, p 187 "Instructions from the New England Company to Gov Endicott in 1629 (Gov Eaton being a member of the company) If any of the savages pretended rights of inheritance to all or any part of the land granted in our patent We pray you endeavor to purchase their title that we may avoid the least scruple of intervension Particularly publish that no wrong or any injury be offered to the natives"

Gov Eaton's Company in purchase of Quinniapiac respected the pretended rights of these Indians, and "in Newman's barn laid down Scripture foundation for the town" from the dwellings assigned them by the English, they were allowed to repair to the English plantation for shelter, and the English were pledged in any just cause to aid in defending them from wrong or harm. The reservation of land for these Indians was made in good faith as the subsequent history of the land purchased from them by the planters show, and considering the values of that time the Indians were amply paid by the descendants of the settlers when the purchase of their reservation was made, such being made by Commissioners of the General Court of Connecticut soon after the year 1715.

INDIAN DEEDS OR TREATIES OF THE PLANTATION OF NEW HAVEN

Articles of agreement betweene Theophilus Eaton & John Davenport & others, English planters att Quinopiocke on the one partye & Momaugin ye Indian Sachem of Quinopiocke & Sugcogisin, Quesaquauch, Caroughood, Wesaucucke & others of his counsell on the partye, made & concluded the 24th of November 1638. Thomas Stanton being interpreter.

That hee ye said sachem, his counsell & company doe jointly profess affirme & covent, (th) at he ye sd Momaugin is the sole sachem of Quinopiocke, and hath an absoluts and independant power to give, alien, dispose or sell, all or any part of the lands in Quinopioske, & that though he have a son now absent, yet neither his sd son, nor any other pson whatsoever hath any right title or interest in any part of the sd lands, soe that whatsoever he, ye fore named sachem, his counsell & ye rest of the Indians present doe & conclude, shall stand firme & inviolable against all claimes & prsons whatsoever.

Secondly ye sd sachem, his counsell & company, amongst which there was a squaw called Shampishuh sister to ye sachem, whoe either had or ptended some interest in some part of ye land, remembering & acknowledging the heavy taxes & eminent dangers wch they lately felt & feared from ye Pequotts, Mohauks, & other Indians, in regard of which they durst not stay in their country, but were forced to flie, & to seeke shelter under the English at Conecticutt, and observing ye safety & ease yt other Indians enjoy neare ye English, of which benefitt they have had a comfortable tast already since the English, began to build & plant at Quinopiocke, which with all thankfullness they now acknowledge. They jointly & freely gave & yeilded up all yr right, title & interest to all ye land rivers & ponds, trees with all ye libertyes & appurtenances belonging unto ye same in Quinopiocke to ye utmost of their bounds East, West, North, South unto Theophilus Eaton, John Davemport & others, the prsent English planters there, & to their heires & assignes for ever, desiring from ym ye sd English planters to receive such a portion of ground on the East side of the Harbour towards ye fort at ye mouth of ye river of Conecticott as might be sufficient for them, being but few in number, to plant in, and yet within these limits to be hereafter assigned to them, they did covent & freely yeild up unto ye said English all the meadow ground lieing therein with full liberty to chuse & cut downe what timber they please, for any use whatsoever, without any question, licence or consent to he asked from them ye sd Indians, and if, after their portion & place be limited & set out by the English as above, they ye sd Indians shall desire to remove to any other place within Quinopiocke bounds, but without ye limitts assigned them, that they doe it not without leave, neither setting up any wigwam, nor breaking up any ground to plant corne, till first it be sett (ou)tt & appointed by ye forenamed English planters for them

Thirdly ye said sachem, his counsell & company desireing liberty to hunt & fish (withi)n the bounds of Quinopiocke now given & graunted to the English as before, doe (hereby) jo(in)tly covent & bind themselves to sett noe traps neare any place where ye (——) whether horses, (ox)en, kine, calves, sheep, goates, hoggs or any sort (

. to take)

any fish out of any ware belonging to any English, nor to doe any thing neare any such ware as to di(sturb) or affright away any fish to ye prjudice of such ware or wares; & that upon discovery of inconveni(en)cy growing to ye English by the Indians disorderly hunting, then hunting shalbe regulated and limited for the prventing of any inconvenience, & yet with as litle damage as to ye Indians in their hunting as may be

Fourthly, ye sd sachem, his counsell & company doe hereby covenant and bind themselves yt none of them shall henceforth hanker about any of ye English houses at any time when the English use to meete about the publique worship of God nor on ye Lords day henceforward bee seene within ye compass of ye English towne, beareing any burdens, or offring to truck with ye English for any comodity whatsoever, & yt none of ym henceforward without leave, open any latch belonging to any English mens dore, nor stay in any English house after warneing that he should leave the same, nor doe any violence, wrong, or injury to ye pson of ye English whether men, women or child, upon any prtence whatsoever, and if English of this plantation, by ymselves or cattle, doe any wrongg or damage to ye Indians, upon complaint just recompence shalbe made by ye English, and yt none of ym henceforward use or take any English mans boate or canoe of what kind soever from ye place where it was fastened or layd, without leave from the owner first haf & obtayned, nor yt they come into ye English towne wth bowes & arrowes, or any other weapons whatsoever in number above 6 Indyans soe armed at a time

Fiftly ye sd sachem, his counsell & company doe truly covenant & bind ymselves yt if any of ym shall hereafter kill or hurt any English cattle of wt sort soever, though casually or negligently, they shall give full satisfaction for the loss or damage as the English shall judge equall, But if any of ym for any respect wilfully doe kill or hurt any of the English cattle, upon proofe they shall pay ye double valew, And if, at any time, any of them find any of the English cattle straying or lost in the woods, they shall bring them backe to the English plantation, & a moderate price or recompence shalbe allowed for their paynes, provided, if it can be proved yt any of ym drove away any English cattle wheresoever they find them, further from ye English plantation to make an increase) or advantage, or recompence for his paynes finding or bringing ym back, they shall in any such case pay damages for such dealings

Sixthly, the number of ye Quinopyocke Indians, me(n) or youth growne to statue fit for service being forty-seven at present they doe covenant and bind ymselves not to receive, or admitt any other Indians amongst them without leave first had & obtayned from ye English? & that they will not, at any time hereafter, entertaine or harbor any that are enemies to ye English, but will psently aprhend such & deliver ym to ye English, and if they know or heare of any plott by ye Indians or others against ye English they will forthwith discover & make ye same known to ym, & in case they doe not, to be accounted as partyes in ye plott, and to be proceeded against as such

Lastly ye sd sachem, his councell & company doe hereby promise truly & carefully to observe & keepe all & every one of these articles of agreemt, & if any of ym offend in any of ye prmisses, they jointly hereby subject and submitt such offendor or offendors to ye consideration, censure & punishmt of the English magestrate or officers appointed among them for goverment without expecting yt ye English should first advise with ym about it, yet in such case of punishmt, if the sd sachem shall desire to know the reason & equity of such pceedings hee shall truly be informed of the same

The former article being read & interprted to ym, they by way of exposition desire yt in ye sixth article it might be added, that if any of the English cattle be killed or hurt casually, or negligently, & proofe made it was done by some of the Quinopiocke Indyans, they will make satisfaction, or if done by any other Indyans, in their sight, if they doe not discober it, & if able to bring ye offendor to ye English they wilbe accounted & dealt with as guilty

In consideration of all which, they desire from ye English, that if at any time hereafter they be affrighted in their dwellings assigned by the English unto ym as before, they may repayre to the English plantation for shelter, & that ye English will there in just cause endeavor to defend ym from wronge But in any quarrel, or warres which they shall undertake, or have wth other Indyans upon any occasion wtsoever, they will manage their affayres by ymselves without expecting any ayd from the English

And the English planters before mentioned accepting and graunting according to ye tenor of the prmises, doe further of their owne accord, by way of free & thankefull retribution, give un(to) ye sachem, counsell & company of ye Quinopiocke Indians, twelve coates of English trucking cloath, twelve alcumy spoones, twelve hatchetts, twelve hoes, two dozen of knives, twelve porengers & foure cases of French knives and sizers, All which being thankfully accepted by ye aforesd & ye agreements in all points perfected, for rettification & full confirmation of the same, the Sachem his counsell & sister, to these prsents have sett their hands or markes ye day & year above written.

Momaugin his marke.

Sugcogisin his marke.

Quesaquaush his mark.

Carroughood his marke.

Weesauenck his mark

Shaumpishuh her marke

On the 11th of December, 1638, Governor Eaton and the other English planters at Quinnypiock "on ye one part and Mantowese sonne of an Indian Sachem living at Mattabeseck (Middletown) and nephew to Seguin on ye other part," made and concluded the second treaty.

Articles of agreement betwixt Theophilus Eaton, John Davenport, & sundry other English planters at Quinnypiock on ye one part and Mantowese sonne of an Indyan sachem liveing at Mattabezeck, and nephew to Sequin on ye other part, made & concluded the 11th day of Decembr 1638.

Firts ye sd Mantowese in prsence & wth allowance and consent of Sawseunck an Indyan wch came in company wth him, doth profess, affirm and covenant, to & wth ye sd Theophilus Eaton, John Davenport & others above, that ye land on both sides the river Quinnypiock from ye Northerly bounds of ye land lately purchased by the sd English of ye Quinnypiock Indyans, namely from ye pond in ye great meadow, about two miles above ye great hill, to ye head of ye river at ye great plaine towards ye plantations settled by ye English upon ye river Quintecutt Southerly, which is about tenn miles in length from north to south, the bounds of which land run alsoe eight miles easterly from ye river of Quinnypiock towards ye river of Quinticutt, and ffive miles westerly towards Hudsons river. doth truely & solely belong to him ye sd Mantowese in right of his deceased mother, to whom ye sd land did appertaine, & from whom it justly descends upon him as his inheritance, soe yt he hath an absolute & independant power to give, alien, dispose or sell all or any part of sd land, as he shall think good, and yt neither his father, nor any other pson whatsoever, have any right title or interest in any part of ye land described and limited as above, whereby he or any other may hereafter justly question what ye sd Mantowese now doth, or lay any clayme to any part of ye sd land now disposed of by him

Secondly the sd Mantowese being fully acquainted wth ye agreemts lately passed betwixt ye sd Englis planters & ye sachem of Quinnypiock, his counsell & company, did freely of his ownes accord upon full & serious deliberation give, grant & yeild up all his right and interest to all ye lands mentioned and bounded as above with all the rivers, ponds, trees, and all liberties & apputenances whatsoever belonging to ye same, to the sd Theophilus Eaton, John Davemport and other English planters att Quinnypiock and to their heyres & assignes for ever, dessireing from them, the sd English planters, to receive such a small portion of land by the rivers side about two miles beyond ye tree over ye river in th passage from hence towards ye townes at Quintecutt, as may be sufficent for his small company being but tenn men in number, besides women and children, wch portion of land they desire may hereafter upon a view, be assigned, appointed and limited unto them by ye sd English planters, reserving alsoe to himselfe and his forenamed company liberty in fitt seasons & due manner without prjudice to ye English upon to hunt, & fish, & kill beaver, yet therein alsoe to be regulated by ye sd English upon discovery of any annoyance, as the Quinnypiock Indyans are in that case

Lastly the said Theophilus Eaton, John Davemport &c accepting from Mantowese this free gift of his hand as above, doe by way of thankfull retribution give unto him eleven coates made of trucking cloth, and one coate for himselfe of English cloth, made up after the English maner, wch being thankfully accepted by the sd Mantowese, and the agreements in all points pfected, for ratificatio and full confirmation of ye same, Mantowese and Sawseunck have hereunto sett their hand or markes the day and year before mentioned

Mantowese 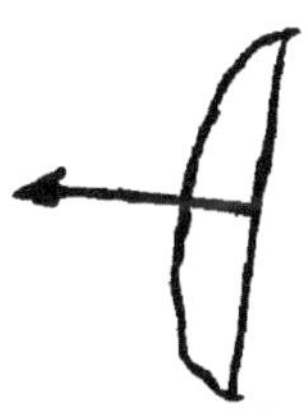 his mrke

Sawseunck  his mrke

I, John Clarke, being interpreter in this treatie, doe hereby professe in the presence of God that I have fully acquainted the Indyans with the substance of every article, to ye wch they have freely agreed that is to say yt Mantowese have given to Mr Davenport & Mr Eaton all his land wch he had by his deceased mother, wch he saith is from ye head of ye great playne to the pond wch he profese to be his, & promise to make it good to or English, & for this hee is satisfyed with twelve coats, onely reserve a piece of land by the river for his men which are 10 and many sqaws to plant in & when or cowes come there what harme their doggs doe to or cattle, they will satisfye for, and we for what harme or doggs doe to them in corne, & as for hunting & fishing, to be free to them as orselves, provided or cattle suffer not by them, & with these particulars they are acquainted, & doe freely consent to them, as their marke wittness, the truth of which, if lawfully called, I shall readily confirme by my oath at any time

per me John Clarke

We Robert Coggswell, Roger Knapp and James Love doe hereby renounce all right to any & every part of the fore mentioned land Wittness our hands hereunto

Robert Coggswell
James Love
Roger Knapp his mrke

See facsimile of treaties in Appendix

On Oct 28, 1639, the civil affairs of the plantation being settled, the planters took an early occasion to apprehend criminals, among whom was an Indian named Nepaupuck, who had formerly been accused of murderously shedding the blood of some of the English

The accused came of his own accord, with a deer's head upon his back, to Mr Eaton's, where, by warrant, the Marshal, Lieut Seely, apprehended and pinioned him, but with the assistance of another Indian he nearly escaped He was, however, retaken and was delivered to the magistrate, by whose orders the prisoner was safely kept in the stocks "till he might be brought to a tryal" The Indian who had assisted in his escape was whipped by the deputy marshal

On October 28, 1639, the Quinnipiack Indian sagamore, and divers of his Indians with him, were examined before the magistrate and the deputies for the plantation, concerning Nepaupuck. They generally accused him of having murdered one or more of the English, and averred that he had cut off the hands of some of them and presented these bloody gifts to Sassacus, the Pequot Sachem, boasting that he had killed the victims with his own hands Mewhebato, a Quinnipiack Indian, kinsman to the aforesaid Nepaupuck, coming at the same time to intercede for him, was examined as to what he knew of the murder charged upon the same Nepaupuck At first he pretended ignorance, but with a distressed countenance and in a trembling manner, being severely admonished to speak the truth, he did acknowledge him guilty according to the charge the other Indians had before made

All the other Indians withdrawing, Nepaupuck was brought in and examined He confessed that Nepaupuck was guilty according to the tenure of the former charge, but denied that he was Nepaupuck, Mewhebato being brought in, he, after some signs of sorrow, charged him to his face that he had assisted the Pequots in murdering the English This somewhat abated his spirit and boldness But Wattonne, the son of Carrahoode, a counsellor to the Quinnipiack Indian sagamore Momaugin, coming in, charged him more particularly that he had killed Abraham Finch, an Englishman, at Wethersfield, and that he himself, the said Wattonne, stood upon the island at Wethersfield and beheld him, the said Nepaupuck now present, acting the same murder

Later, the Quinnipiack sagamore and the rest of the Indians being called in, to his face affirmed that the accused was Nepaupuck and that he had murdered one or more of the English as before Nepaupuck, then finding that a denial was of no use, confessed that he was Nepaupuck, and boasted that he was a great captain, had murdered Abraham Finch and others He said he knew that he must die and was not afraid, and laid his neck on the mantel tree of the chimney, desiring that his head might be cut off, or that he might die in any other way the English should appoint Only he said fire was God and God was angry with him, therefore he would not fall into God's hands He was then returned to the stocks and a watch put over him

The next day, October 29th, a criminal court being assembled to proceed against the said Indian, Nepaupuck, he was brought to "the barre" He denied that he was the Nepaupuck which had committed the murder which he was charged with, when he saw that the Quinnipiack sagamore and the Indians did again accuse him to his face he confessed but said there was a Mohawk Indian of that name, who had killed more than he

Wattonne affirmed to his face that the said Nepaupuck did not only kill Abraham Finch, but was one of them that had killed the three men in a boat on Connecticut River, and that there was but one Nepaupuck, and that the accused was he, and the same that took a child of Mr Swaine's at Wethersfield Then the said Nepaupuck being asked if he would not confess that he had deserved to die, he answered, "It is weregin"* (sic)

The Court having such convincing proof against the prisoner, proceeded to pass sentence upon him according to the nature of the fact and the rule of the Mosaic law, "He that sheds man's blood by man shall his blood be shed"

Accordingly the prisoner's head was cut off the next day and it was pitched on a pole in the market place, and exhibited as the skulls of criminals were displayed (as shown in prints of that date) on the gate towers of London Bridge

At a General Court held January 4th, 1639, with other business, it was ordered that no planter or planters shall make purchase of any land or plantation from the Indians or others for their own private use or advantage, but, *in the name, and for the use of the whole plantation*

At a General Court held the 23rd of the eighth month, 1640, land was laid out between Mr Davenport's farm and the Indian wigwams on the east side (Quinnipiac River, "Dragon Bank") and Mr Gregson (who petitioned for land at Solitary Cove in 1639 and then was allotted August 5th, 1644, 133 acres) was appointed truckmaster of the town for the ensuing year, to truck with the Indians for venison, so that he might sell, as the records have it, "to the planters that have need at 3d per pound and it is ordered that wampum (shell money) shall go in this plantation, 6 for a penny'

Again, as noted in the records November 29th, 1641, "It is ordered that Wequash [a Niantic chief] shall have a suit of clothes made at the town's charge" This Wequash was an Indian living at the mouth of the Connecticut River He was often at Saybrook with Mr Fenwick He became a preacher to the Indians, but died suddenly ("very comfortably"), and the note says "Not without suspicion of poison"

* Fine things, ornaments, etc , etc —DeForest p 497

In 1642 there was an Indian war scare, and the General Court held September 17th ordered as follows: "When an alarm is made every soldier shall repair to the meeting house forthwith &c and it is ordered in case of any expedition against the Indians, whom the Captain shall see fit to set forth upon service, they shall go forthwith without any further dispute, though it shall be at extreme hazard of their lives; and if any man refuses, the magistrate is to press him to go whether he will or not"

"At a General Court held the 6th of July, 1643, articles of Confederation betwixt the Plantations of Massachusetts, Plymouth, Connecticut, and New Haven, (which were concluded at Boston, May 19, 1643) were read and by the whole Court approved and confirmed; and it was ordered that the Secretary enter them as a record, and it was agreed 'How all the jurisdictions may carry it towards the Indians' 'That they neither grow insolent or be injured without due satisfaction, lest war break in upon the Confederates through such miscarriages'"

This abstract is given to show that the natives were allowed to have their respective rights, which were recognized by the United Colonies

The Confederacy lasted until Winthrop obtained the Connecticut Charter When New Haven was consolidated with Connecticut Colony it was dissolved The Confederacy was called "The United Colonies of New England," and a most important Confederation it was.

At a General Court held the 14th of October, 1643, it was ordered that "six men shall forthwith be sent from hence to join with eight of Connecticut to assist Uncas against the Narragansett Indians, whom he expects shortly to war upon him, and accordingly to be fitted and furnished with all necessaries for such a voyage and enterprise"

The Commissioners of the United Colonies having at their September session in Boston decided upon delivering up Miantonomo to be put to death by Uncas, were apprehensive that the Narragansetts would seek to revenge his death The records further say "On the 27th of October following, the Court considering that six soldiers being sent forth to join with eight soldiers from Hartford for Uncas' defense against the assault which may be made upon him by the Narragansett Indians for Miantonamo's death which with the shallop attending them will be a further charge to this jurisdiction "*

A letter from Mr Ludlow was read in Court May 25, 1644, about the Indians having cruelly murdered an Englishman between Stamford and Unkaway Hoping to procure the murderers, Mr Ludlow had caused seven Indians to be apprehended, but the Indians had risen in great company about the town and thus put the inhabitants in fear Therefore Mr Ludlow desired advice what to do Whereas it was ordered to detain the Indians prisoners, and if help was needed, twenty men to be sent forthwith

A letter from Thurston Raynor reporting that a woman had been cruelly murdered by an Indian, was read in Court June 3, 1644, and at a General Court held the 19th of August the same year, Captain Turner and Mr Malbon were chosen deputies for the Court to be held for this jurisdiction about the tryal of an Indian called Busheage.

The prisoner had been arrested and delivered to the English by Wirchborough, a Potatuck Indian The record of the trial is lost, but Winthrop informs us that "the magistrate of New Haven taking advice of the Elders in those parts and some here, did put him to death" "The executioner struck off his head with a falchion, but he had eight blows before he could effect it, and the Indian sat upright and stirred not all the time"

On account of another Indian scare a Court was held on the 20th of June 1645, which found that there was need of sending forth soldiers to strengthen Uncas against the Narragansett Indians, etc It was ordered that the governor with the

* Uncas, chief of the Mohegans, claimed title by conquest as far as Guilford, eastern bounds, and Foxon Wigwam at Stoney River two miles above the village crossing, perhaps a hunting outpost of this Mohegan chief within the Quinnipiack region, where in the cattle path his people set traps, and in 1644 the Marshal was sent from New Haven to warn Uncas or his brother about it This brother, like Uncas, a Mohegan, held sway here in lieu of tribute The best authorities brand Uncas as a bloodthirsty, drunken wreck, the murderer of Miantonomo, and making use of every means in his power to prevent the efforts of the English from advancing civilization among the Indians

4

rest of the Court with the captain and lieutenant as a council of war, should dispose and order all military affairs until the General Court should settle some course concerning the same

At the next Court, held August 18, 1645, it was desired "That some course might be taken for the general safety owing to these rumors and tumults of the Indians The Gunsmith was ordered to repair those guns which are defective" Henry Peck and Old Bassett were desired to set the great guns on good strong carriages Farmers were to keep butter and cheese on hand in case the public service required it Those who went to the woods and meadows to work were to keep near each other and to carry their arms, and it was desired that two should go with every herd (to watch) on the Lord's days

On the 25th of August following the General Court took under consideration the unprotected state of the farms, and it was advised that a good watch be kept, and it was propounded that those that had guns should lend them to the soldiers that were to go abroad, also those with shoes and stockings to spare were to furnish them to the soldiers, and Mr Gregson was to see them satisfied

This year (1645) it was ordered that wampum should go for current pay in the plantation in any payment under twenty shillings "if half be black and half be white," "and in case any question shall arise about the badness of any wampum, Mr Goodyeare shall judge if they repair to him "*

* Wampum or wampum-peague, English, sewan, Dutch, the name of Indian money made in the shape of beads from the white and purple of the quogue or round clam shell, dates back to the time of the Mound Builders [1] The American Indians used it as a medium for trade barter, tribute and ransom, and in time it came into use by the European settlers of the northeastern part of the North American continent The wampum made by the Indians of Connecticut and Long Island was flatt and round, measuring about a sixteenth of an inch thick and one-eighth of an inch long, and was strung alternately white and purple on a native hemp thread, and when used for ornament was stitched to their buckskin garments by means of a needle made from the sharp bone of a wild fowles leg It was also stitched to their wampum belts and zigzaged between representations of stars, animals and implements of peace and war

[1] Wampum peague, an Algonquin word signifying white sewan or money

The Quinnipiacks, after a few years contact with the settlers, appear to have made some progress towards civilization and

The Narragansett and Long Island Indians were the greater producers of wampum or sewan, and on account of the production and manufacture of these shells Long Island was called Sewanhacky or "the land of shells" This Indian money was made by drilling holes through the thickest part of the white and purple clam shells by means of a spear or arrow shaft, pointed with flint or agate, and rapid motions imparted to the shaft by several turns around it with an unstrung bow string, and the primitive drilling powers was used also by them to light their fires, and the shells once drilled were broken down to small sizes, then ground with stone to give a uniform shape

In 1637 wampum was made a legal tender in Connecticut for any amount and was received for taxes at "foursin (4) a penny, and so much bad peague was thrown upon the market that the Commissioners of the United Colonies of New England were applied to for a remedy and they recommended to the seperate colonial governments to suppress this poor peage" by law, and in March 1649, the General Court of Connecticut ordered that no peague, white or black, be paid or received but what is strung suitably and not small and great, uncomely and disorderly mixed, as formerly it hath been

The accepted length of a string of wampum was the fathom containing 360 beads valued at 10 shillings each fathom This shell money in 1645 was ordered by the Court to pass, "the black or purple for 8 a penny, and the white at 6 a penny, but in April 1650, much of the wampum that is brought (probably for taxes) is so faulty that ye officers can hardly or not at all pass it away" It was reckoned in July 1657, at 6 shillings 8 pence per fathom In November 1657, it was ordered that all payment with the church treasury be in silver or bills, and in December 1656, it was voted by this General Court that ' seeing Wumpum is a drugg Harriman the keeper of the ordinary (site New Haven hotel) might refuse it" The importance of it is illustrated by the fact that the Dutch West India Company in 1664 sought to negotiate a loan of five (5) or six (6) thousand guilders in it where with to pay the labouring people, the obligations to be satisfied with good negroes or goods. In July 1673, New York was drained of wampum by its being sent West for Indian trade, and to remedy this the government by a proclamation in 1672 commanded that "Instead of 8 white and 4 black beads 6 white and 3 black should pass as a stiver and three times so much the value of silver"—Hazzard's *Annuals of Penn*

About this date 8 beads of white was valued equal to one (1) stiver, and twenty (20) stivers to four (4) pence sterling or six (6) pence currency, which equalled one (1) guilder

Purchase of land treaties and ransoms between the Indians and Colonies continued to be satisfied by exchange of wampum belts, and the last that we have any knowledge of it was at Prairie du Chein in 1825 [1]

[1] There are still in the possession of the Lion Gardiner and Townsend families two ancient wampum treaty belts.

had copied the English mode of cultivating their land These lands were located near the village on their reservation on the east side, but the Indians having a desire to live near the English, they presented a petition to the General Court 24th, 2d month (April), 1657, concerning which the governor acquainted the town, when a meeting was held, that "The occasion of this meeting is about the Indians"

"They say," continued the governor, "they have not land enough on the other side to plant on and they desire they might hire some of the English lands about Oyster Point and plant there, where they also desire to dwell this summer if they may have liberty, and they have promised that they will not be injurious to the English and that they will not work on the Sabbath day,' etc

Much debate was had in the matter, and in the issue it was referred to the Particular Court and the townsmen were to treat with the petitioners as they should see cause Only these conditions were required by the town to be observed, viz —

"That they harbor no strange Indians to dwell with them, that they kill all their dogs, some of which had done much mischief already, that they neither burn or spoil any man's fence, nor cut wood upon any man's ground without leave, nor take any wood already cut, as some of them have done, if they do, just satisfaction will be required, also that they stay not late in the town at night, nor come into the town with any arms, hatchets, clubs, &c, and that they come not into any house without asking leave, and if they are bid to go away that they do it without gainsaying"

Accordingly the Committee met and treated with the sagamore and some other Indians deputed for the occasion, who after consideration returned answer, that the Indians would not kill their dogs They were then told that they must remove to their own land on the other side

During numerous visits to England I have spared neither time nor expense, copying and photographing from original documents and from the Rev Abraham Pierson's Catechism in the British Museum, material of the Quinnipiack Indians for publication,* and while unavoidably delayed, this work has been accomplished and explained in a most scholarly style by

* See Appendix

an able expert, Mr Wilberforce Eames of the Lenox Library and printed in 1891 by the Smithsonian Institute of Ethnology, edited by J C Pilling, Major J. N Powell, Director, from which I have made copious abstracts of what has seemed to me of interest regarding this translation of the language of this tribe who sold their "pretended right" to this region to Gov Theophilus Eaton, and his settlers in 1638, as the deeds or treaties abundantly testify The earliest reference to Mr Pierson's work among the Quinnipiacks appears in a letter from the Commissioners of the United Colonies of New England to the Corporation in England for the Propagation of the Gospel amongst the Indians in New England, dated at New Haven, Sept 10th, 1651, in which they wrote that "Mr Leveridge, Mr Blinman, and Mr Pierson are studying the language that they may the better treat with them concerning things of their peace" In another letter dated Sept 12th of the same year and addressed to Mr Eliot [the Apostle] they wrote "Mr Higginson (of Guilford) hath spent some time formerly about the Indian language and Mr Pierson hath done the like and continuith with much seriousness therein"

In September 1653 Mr Rawson was ordered by the Commissioners to pay Mr Pierson of Branford within New Haven jurisdiction the sum of twelve (12) pounds towards his charges, and pains in fitting himself to teach the Indians, and in September 1654 it was agreed that Mr Pierson for his pains and charges and fitting himself for the Indian works shall be paid fifteen (15) pounds out of the Corporation Stock

The Commissioners wrote to the Corporation in London Sept 25th 1654 in reference to Mr Eliot's work among the Indians as follows: "One catechism is already printed and Mr. Pierson is preparing another to suite these Southwest parts (Quinnipiack) where the language differs from those who live about Massachusetts At their meetings in New Plymouth two (2) years later in Sept 1656, a letter from Mr Pierson of Branford dated the 25th August last was read and some parts of a Catechisme by him framed and propounded to convince the Indians by the light of nature and reason that there is only one God who has made, and knoweth all things, was considered and the Commissioners advised that it be perfected and turned into the Narragansett or Pequot language that it may be the better understood by the Indians in all parts of the country, and for the purpose they spake with and desired Tho Stanton to advise with Mr Pierson about a fitt season to meet and translate the same accordingly, without any unnecessary delay that it might be fitted for and sent to the press and they promised him due satisfaction for his time and pains It was agreed that Mr Pierson bee allowed fifteen (15) pounds for his pains hee shall take in this work the year insuing"

The Catechism was completed and a copy transcribed for the press before the next meeting of the Commissioners in Sept 1657 when they wrote to the Corporation on the 19th of that month that "wee have also improved his (Mr Stanton's) skill in helping Mr Pierson an able and usful instrument for other Indians spiritual good in translating a Catichisme Mr Pierson hath made for their use and instruction and as the account will show have given him a suitable allowance—Wee have also sent you—Mr Pierson's Cattachisme which we have desired Mr Ince to transcribe whome you may please to improve to overlook the press to prevent mistakes especially of the Indians wee desire the worke may be expedited, and that 1500 coppies bee sent hither to us by the first opportunity" This Catechism however never reached England, as the ship which carried it was lost at sea with all on board

The Corporation replied to the Commissioners April 30th 1658 "As for Mr Pierson wee concure with you concerning his fitness and abilities for the Indians Spirituall good, and for the Catechismes mentioned in your letter of his* composing for their use and instruction which we should have taken care to have printed according to your desire and should be sent over the number mentioned in your letter; but we fear it is miscarried being sent as we understand in Mr Garrett's shipp which is yet missing, and therefore we intreate you to send it over by the first opportunity"

On the 16th of Sept 1658 the Commissioners wrote to the Corporation that "Mr Pierson, wee here is repairing his Catichisme for the press and is expected heer every day; We hope

* Letter sent by Garrett's ship with Thomas Mayhew and Jonathan Ince both lost on passage to London from Boston

to send it to you by the next, together with this years acts which as yet we have not had time to perfect," and again in a letter dated from Boston September 22, 1658, they added "By our last of the 16th instant we certifyed you of our purpose to send Mr Pierson Catichisme by the first opportunity to bee printed in England Since which time it is come to our hands, but upon further consideration in regard of the hazard of sending and dificulties of the printing if without a fitt overseer of the press by one skilled in the language we have chosen rather to have it printed heer and accordingly have taken order for same, and hope it wilbee finished within three (3) months"

The printing was not begun probably until two (2) or three (3) months later, as only the first sheets (sixteen (16) pages including the title) had been "wrought of the presse" of Samuel Green at Cambridge when the ship by which a specimen was sent to England sailed from Boston at the end of December of the same year This specimen sheet was reprinted for the Corporation in their report entitled "A further account of the Progress of the Gospel amongst the Indians in New England" which was published in London before May 1659

Although the title of the Cambridge Editions is dated 1658 the impression of the Catechism was not finished until the autumn or winter of the next year On the 7th of May 1659 the Corporation wrote to the Commissioners "Concerning your printing Mr Pierson's Catechisme in the Indian language in New England wee concurr with your judgment therein, conceiving you have ordered it for the best, In regard that such errors as may bee committed in printing the same wilbee better corrected there, than they would be heer —Wee have thought good to print your letter with two (2) other letters received from Mr Endicott and Mr Elliott, as also the Indian exortations and also the sheet of Catechisme composed by Mr Pierson all which are printed for publick satestaction"

To this letter the Commissioners replied from Hartford September 7th 1659 We have ordered Mr Usher to send you forty (40) copies of Mr Piersons Cattichisme if finished before the ship setts sayle but fear by reason of Mr Piersons sickness the work may have been retarded and we and you suffer a disapointment but we shall endeavor by the next to satisfy your expectations therein In the account of charges sent with this letter was one item of 40 pounds to Mr Green for printing the Psalms and Mr Pierson's Catachisme

At the meeting held in New Haven in September 1660 it was resolved that the Commissioners for Massachusetts are desired and impowered to accoumpt with Mr Green for the forty (40) pounds paid him the last year on account for printing Mr Pierson's Cattachisme and the Psalms; the Treasurers account of "Indian Stock" submitted at their next meeting at Plymouth in September 1661 contains an entry of five (5) pounds discount with Mr Green over paid on account of printing Mr Pierson's Catechisme The present knowledge of the fact that this Catechisme is not in the Narragansett or Pequot dialect of Eastern and Southern Connecticut as might be inferred from the letter and records of the Commissioners but in that of the *Quinnipi or Southwestern Indians of the same colony is due entirely to the learned research of Dr Trumbull* The salary paid by the Commissioners to Mr Pierson for his labour in instructing the Indians was raised from fifteen (15) to twenty (20) pounds in 1657 and again to thirty (30) pounds in 1661 but at the meeting in September 1667 his allowance for services during the year was lowered to fifteen (15) pounds, probably on account of his removal from Branford

In 1665, when New Haven Colony was joined to Connecticut, Mr Pierson removed to Newark, New Jersey, with some of his Branford friends and made settlements there in June 1667, and dying August 9, 1678* was succeeded in the ministry by his son Abraham Pierson Jr, who afterward became the first rector of Yale College The Reverend Abraham Pierson Sr was born probably in Yorkshire, England, about the year, 1608 graduated at Trinity College, Cambridge, and preached at Newark, Co Nottingham Emigrated to Boston

* The Rev Abraham Pierson of Branford wrote on the death of Governor Eaton an Elegy of 38 lines to express his sorrow See Mass Hist Coll, Vol VII, Series IV, p 477

"Eaton so famed, so wise, so meek, so just,
The Phoenix of our world here hides his dust,
His name forget [New Haven] never must"

1639 or 40 In a letter to Daniel Gookin dated Nov 20th, 1674, the Reverend James Fitch, Sr (a son in law of the Rev Henry Whitfield of Guilford), who had preached to the Indians living near him, wrote of the result of Mr Pierson's labours as follows: "Concerning the Indians in this colony, Connecticut and at Long Island I cannot understand that they have any inclination to learn the knowledge of God, but when Mr. Pierson did frequently try in the several plantations in the colony they did generally show an aversment yea a perverce contempt for the word of God and at present they will not yield to any settled hearing or attendance upon the ministery of the word"* This mention of Mr Pierson has been made to preserve facts and assist others while in search of Quinnipiack history

From this date, 1657, to the breaking out of King Philip's War, June, 1675, only casual mention is made in our records of the Quinnipiack tribe, although there was fear expressed at the General Court Nov 23d, 1663 Mr Jones propounded about the great guns both at the water side and meeting house

This Indian uprising [King Philip's War], which had been impending for several years, received a crushing blow in the defeat of the Narragansett Indians, December 19th, 1675 This tribe, it will be remembered, had broken their treaty with the English of Plymouth and had allied themselves with Philip, Chief of the Wamponaogs, to exterminate the English The fight was called the "Direful Swamp Fight," and

* In New Haven Colony Records 1646, page 262, in support of this give the following

"Pawquash a Quillipiock Indian was first complayned of for leaving open the Oyster Shell gate and damadge being done thereby refused to give any satisfaction"

"He about four years since came into Mr Craynes House when they were blessing God in the name of Jesus Christ, and that he then did blaspheamously say that Jesus Christ was 'Mattamoy and naught, and his bones rotten and spake of an Indian in Mantoises plantation ascending into Heaven wch was witnessed by Mr Crayne and others'

"The centence of the Court was that he should be severely whipped for thus scorning at or worshipping God & blaspheme the name of Jesus Christ and he was informed if he should do so hereafter it would hazzard his life."

"And for the damadge by means of the gate he had left open to pay Tho Knowles 5 shilling."

occurred while Philip of Pokonoket, the principal actor, was in winter quarters west of Albany, stirring up the Mohawks and northern tribes to war

The Narragansetts had congregated at a Paliasade Fort in South Kingston Rhode Island This stronghold was located on an island surrounded by a swamp and only approachable during winter frosts

Philip was slain at his seat at Mt Hope, August, 1676 The effect of this war lasted until 1678 among the allied Indians in Maine

At a town meeting held in New Haven the 2d of July, 1675, the town was acquainted by Mr Jones that an uprising and outrages had taken place among the Indians in Plymouth and Swansy, which news came to him from the governor

Everyone able to bear arms was thereupon ordered at once to repair and to be in readiness for service until further news of the trouble was received, and those at the farms were to hold themselves ready for defense, or to come to town

The town was also informed that "our Indians deny all knowledge of Phillip's motion," also that "neither did they like them,' and that they also said "they had no men gone away, and would give the town any intelligence they met with, and if any strange Indians came to them they would inform us and not harbor them"

The town ordered ' that an account be taken of the Indians, how many men there are and where they are" And Matthew Moulthrop, who now took the constable's oath, was warned to look after them

At a town meeting September 24, 1675, a committee was "appointed to consider of, and direct some fortifications at the meeting house and places about town," which was done,* and

* History of Ancient Woodbury—Palisades, p 66 Houses were palisaded in the following manner, viz a deep ditch was dug all around the house, logs were then placed perpendicularly in the ditch all around it, leaving space for a gate Logs sharpened at the top, placed close together, and about twelve (12) feet above the ground The ditch filled in and the earth replaced and stamped down and here part of the ditch open, this with the gate was a good defence against sudden attacks

This is probably the way New Haven meeting house and places about the town were fortified July 2, 1693, Vol II, New Haven Town Records The townsmen desire Mr John Cooper, Sr and Sergeant Dickerman to take down the flankers by the meeting house and secure them

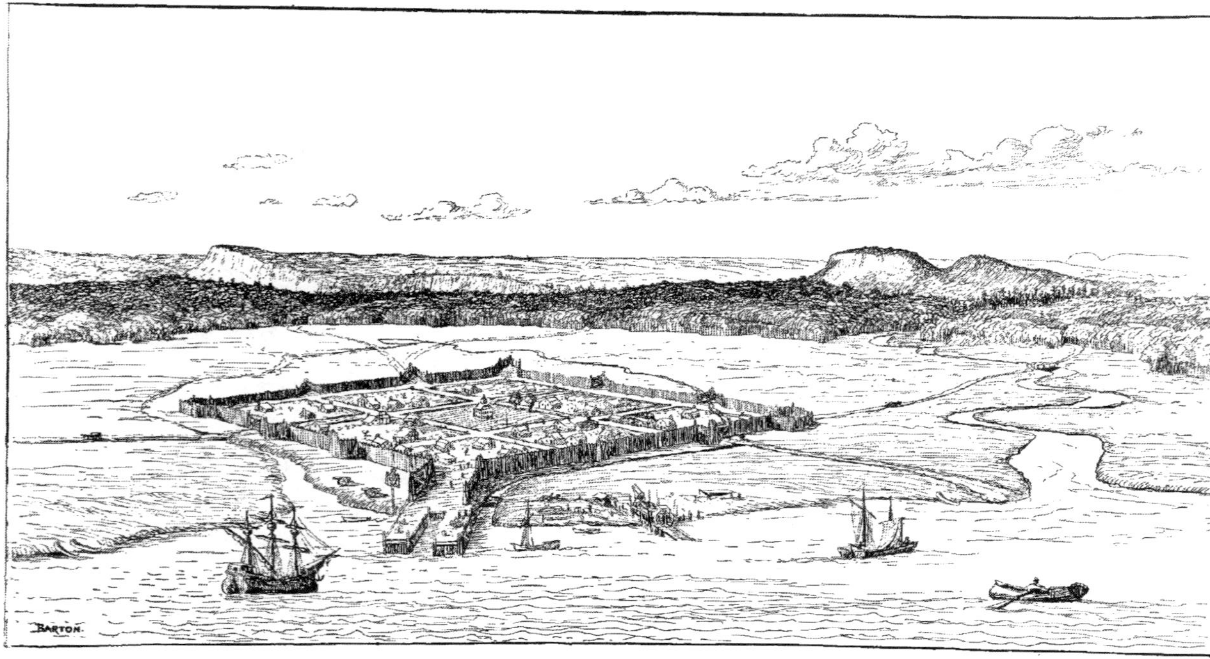

NEW HAVEN FORTIFIED.

KING PHILIP'S WAR, 1675.

Captain Wm Rosewell was ordered to prepare the great guns for service, and all inhabitants to bring their arms to meeting on the Sabbath and other public days

On the 12th of October following, news of the burning of Springfield by the Indians was received, and it was thought best to build fortifications at the end of each street and at the angles of the town, and fortify (palisade) some of the houses (one of which was Mr Harriman's, site of the New Haven House), also to fortify the square of the town with a line of palisades or posts on the sides of the quarters

The records further note that "Upon debate of these things it was ordered that at the end of the streets and at the four angles these fortifications or places of shelter (flankers) against the shot of an enemy should be set up, as the committee shall appoint, and the persons in the town to work freely at it until they are finished"

"It was also ordered that all small brush and brushwood within half a mile of the town plot should be cut down and cleared away that it might not afford shelter to the Indians to creep in a skulking manner near the town" This accounts for the barren flat lands on all sides of the town plot remembered by men now living

On the 18th of October, Major Treat informed the town, saying "The Narragansetts are in preparation for war," and the General Court advised all plantations to fortify themselves the best they can against the common enemy

War was formally declared against the Narragansett Indians on November 2d, 1675, by the United Colonies of New England, and the troops raised by Massachusetts, Plymouth and Connecticut were called the Army of the United Colonies of New England

The Governor of Plymouth Colony, General Josiah Winslow, was appointed commander-in-chief, Major Samuel Appleton commanded the Massachusetts troops, Major William Bradford the Plymouth and Major Robert Treat those of Connecticut The Massachusetts and Plymouth troops, horse and foot, numbered about 700 men They came by land and water to Bull's Garrison House (which they found had been burned just before), at Pettysquamscott, Rhode Island, where they met the Connecticut troops, consisting of about 300 men and 150 Mohegan and Quinnipiac Indians, on Saturday, December 18th, at 5 o'clock in the afternoon, during a heavy snow storm

The military officers in New Haven just previous to King Philip's war were as follows so far as records show, and I regret that I have not been able to find the rolls of the private soldiers In the militia the quota of a full company was sixty-four men which entitled the company to a captain; thirty two members gave right to a lieutenant and twenty-four to a sergeant Each company had two drummers and two fifers

In 1675 the captain of the New Haven company was William Rosewell, and the lieutenant, Thomas Trowbridge

The military officers in New Haven just previous to King Philip's war as shown by the records:

JOHN NASH,	Captain
THOMAS MUNSON,	Lieutenant
JOHN MILES,	Ensign
NATHANIEL MERRIMAN,	Sargeant
SAMUEL WHITEHEAD,	"
ROGER ALLING,	"
JAMES BISHOP,	"

The Connecticut troops killed and wounded in this fight according to

Trumbull		*Hubbard*	
Captain Gallop Co ,	10	New Haven Co ,	20
Marshall,	14	Stratford Co , Seeley,	20
Seeley,	20	Hartford Co , Watts,	14
Mason,	9	Windsor Co , Marshall,	17
Watts,	17		
	70		71

It was voted at this town meeting also to fortify some houses at once, and, at a second vote, that there should be a line of fortifications made about the town

In this war Connecticut's quota was 350 white men together with 150 Mohegan and Quinnipiack Indians The whole were formed into five companies under the command of Major Robert Treat On the following Sunday the troops marched fifteen miles to the swamp They were led by a treacherous Narragansett Indian through a deep snow and arrived at the fort about 1 P M The Massachusetts troops led 527 strong, with Plymouth in the centre, 128 men, and the Connecticut contingent guarding the rear

The fight was long and bloody At length the Connecticut troops under the command of the valiant Maj Robert Treat charged over the logs and rushed into the fort Three hundred Indian warriors perished, three hundred more died of their wounds and from cold, and nearly the same number, together with the women and children, were made prisoners Major Treat* is said to have been the last man to leave the fort Of the Captains, Seeley, Gallop, and Marshall of Connecticut, were killed, and the New Haven company had twenty men slain

The victory was dearly bought Six captains and eighty men were killed or mortally wounded One hundred and fifty of the wounded afterwards recovered

The army, after burning the fort, retired with their dead and wounded about sunset and arrived at their headquarters† at midnight, where the wounded received relief, but the cold weather, the storm and fatigue prevented many from recovering

On the return of the army to Wickford, where the Massachusetts and Plymouth troops went into winter quarters, the Connecticut contingent having suffered a greater loss than the others in officers and men in proportion to their numbers, returned home This action was considered detrimental to the service by the other Colonies

Soon after the return of the New Haven troops, at a town meeting held on the seventh of February, 1675–6, it was voted to finish the fortifications On the 5th of March following, Mr Jones acquainted the meeting that "We had need be quickened into all due means for our safety" Jeremiah Osborn acquainted the town that the Committee for fortifications had met according to former order to oversee and set the work forward, and that they had gotten in all the wood which was ordered from the inhabitants, excepting about 15 loads, and to finish the line on their side they thought it would take

* Major Treat was second in command
† Smith Garrison House

about one hundred loads, and also there were no gates, and without all be finished, things would not be safe John Cooper, Sr, who was the overseer on his side, required one hundred loads to finish his side's work

The records further note "It is ordered that no Indian be suffered to come into the town to see the fortifications or take notice of any of our acts or motions and that, by the constable, warning be given the Indians that not any of them may come into the town, nor unto any English house; and that if any Indian come into the Town he be apprehended and sent back again; yet what may be to avoid any misusing of them"

Mr Augur and Mr Trowbridge gave 20 shillings each towards making the gates, and it was left with the Committee to see that all the gates and fortifications were duly finished

It was also ordered that no person should plant any Indian corn within two rods of the stockade line

At town meeting on the 11th of March following, it was moved as follows: "That all persons able to work on the fortifications, shall set to work when the drum beateth in the morning and anyone that is defaulty shall pay 5 shillings towards the work" A Committee was appointed to regulate the ditching and breast-work and John Nash the gun smith was spared, that he might be beneficial to persons about their arms

On the 25th of April following, at another town meeting, it was ordered "The fortification line about the town shall be finished as soon as the seed can be got into the ground, and that when all the wood shall be supplied, the Committee shall also appoint how the line shall be finished", and the palisades were then probably completed

Early in the year 1677 and in December, 1678, the town ordered, "*On account of peace* all the fortification stuff, whether set up or lying down which is not quarter fence, be sold by the Town for the good of the Town" As there is a record of a sale ordered of fortification wood, January 31st, 1681, it was probably then sold standing, at sixpence a rod, and it is interesting to note that we have recorded proof that New Haven was once fortified with flankers, moat and pales at the Ditch Corner After this war (about 1680) there were two hundred acres of land given in the third division to the soldiers of the Narragansett expedition, as the records of several Connecticut towns show.*

The Colonial Records of New Haven Colony give only a faint outline of the fortifications that were built about the town for protection during King Philip's Wars, but enough has been recorded to give an idea, and the rest must be drawn from imagination.

The fortifications consisted of a palisade line of wooden posts of timber that would square twelve (12) inches set close together five (5) feet in the ground and several thicknesses and ten (10) feet above and at the top pointed, which were properly braced and filled in between with earth and clay excavated from the ditch dug on the outside ten (10) feet deep and fifty (50) feet wide which was flooded with water from the harbor, and perhaps from the Beaver Ponds.

This Palisade was built wide enough for a soldier to march on top and may have had also a platform on the inside low enough for a sentinel to walk, with body protected by the works, with loopholes for observation. On the sea side in full view were the king's arms cut in wood and great guns mounted, also at the meeting house in the Market Place, which was protected by flankers and palisades (with a "watch

* The Canadians frequently stirred up the northern tribes to resume a hostile attitude, and after the King Philip War, the colonists were in constant danger, and in 1689 a flying army stood ready to march at any moment against the Indians. In this war Lt. Amos Talmadge of New Haven was slain and burned, at Schenectady, N. Y., 1690. A patrol of four horsemen was continually scouring the woods and the militia were obliged to carry their arms to meeting. The Quinnipiack Indians were useful as auxiliaries and were employed as scouts. One of these scouts, a Quinnipiack, while watching in the gap at Mullin Hill (East Haven), borrowed a gun of Mr. Hemingway of Stoney river and while on duty saw two of the hostile Indians coming towards him from Pond Rock, and as they passed him while in range he, hoping to kill both at one shot, pulled the trigger, which only "snapped in the pan," [flint lock] not being loaded. Not having been observed by the enemy the Indian escaped with his life. The enemy crossed the Peat Meadows and joined the friendly Indians at Beacon Hill. The enraged warrior threatened to kill Mr. Hemingway for deceiving him as he alleged in order that he might be killed, but when Mr. Hemingway's innocence in the case was proved, the warrior was pacified, but in a day or two one of their spies, as was afterwards proven, was found dead in the Indian fields, and it is supposed he had been killed by this warrior.—Dodd.

tower" on top) Here was kept the armor belonging to the town, an account of which, given in the records, is very interesting The east and west creeks and the harbor flats were dug out at an early date to allow vessels to reach the outskirts of the town plot, and as the records state in the East creek as far as Mr Preston's corner, now State and Chapel streets, where, since the Revolution, I have been told, West India traders have unloaded their cargoes, the Custom House and Post Office and business center was just above, near the junction of State, Elm and Grand streets, the head of navigation The West creek was navigable for boats as far as the corners of College and George street, and the tide has been known to set back in the creek as far as the corner of Park and Chapel street, 'and a ravine continuing to its source, corner of Elm and Howe streets, may still be traced

This divergence is given to show how the creeks may have been dug out to assist in protection from Indian raids, and that ditches might have been excavated from the creeks, meeting at the Ditch Corner out Broadway, an important gateway to the town which was always closed at night and where were located the pales, the last of the Palisades, where young Brewster, when "over come," was found and fined by the Court

The Indian Reservation seems to have been kept intact, as originally laid out, until the year 1679, when at a town meeting held December 29th of that year, several propositions from the inhabitants on the east side were considered One of the propositions was "That they of the village [East Haven] may have liberty to purchase some land of the Indians near Mr Gregson's farm, *if the Indians are willing to sell it*" Other propositions of a like nature were referred to a commission (This was probably at the next meeting)

After the town had heard the consideration of the committee, the town, in answer to the inhabitants, recommended caution, saying "As to the purchase of lands from the Indians near Mr Gregson's farm, New Haven being bound in covenants to supply the Indians with planting lands when they need it, it is questionable how far liberty to purchase lands of them may consist with that engagement and unless with due caution, is to be considered"

The Quinnipiack Indians at this date (1680) seem to have numbered at least one hundred men, and it was thought not expedient to sell their rights to the reservation

Between the years 1680 and 1750 there seems to have been a great diminution of this tribe, occasioned undoubtedly by King Philip's War, 1675, the Canadian War, 1690, the Louisburg expedition, 1745, and the English conquest in the West Indies, where many Quinnipiacks went as soldiers and sailors and died with disease or in battle, the Quinnipiacks having contributed in each of these contests a part of Connecticut's quota, and this loss of men to the tribe may have set again on foot the scheme to buy from them a portion of their tract adjoining the ferries and meadows on the west, and farms on the east Pres Stiles writes that at the time of the Cuban expedition in 1740, there were not more than fifteen or twenty Indian families left in the town

We now quote from the New Haven Town Records, beginning with Vol VI, p 394, when the General Court of the Colony of Connecticut granted the town of New Haven the right to sell Indian lands.

This indenture made the 14th day of September Anno Domini One thousand six hundred and ninety five (1695) betwixt Nayhanatt, alias George Sagamore of New Haven Indians in New England of the one party, and John Morris Thomas Tallmadge, and John Sackett of said New Haven and said New England of the other party, witnesseth, that the said Nayhanatt alias George Sagamour with the full and free consent of Rum Tom, Ombuychoe and Chiefs of his Indians hath devised, granted and letten and by these presents, doth demise, grant and lett unto the said John Morris, Thomas Tallmadge, and John Sackett, a certain tract of land lying in the old Indian field near the Old Ferry, containing by estimation *18* acres, be it more or less, *bounded by the highway that cometh to the said Ferry north*, Mr Thomas Trowbridge, his land *south*, the Indian *fence east*, and said *Ferry west*, with one acre and a half being part of said eighteen acres *lying on the north side of aforesaid highway*, bounded with said *highway southerly* and with said Mr Trowbridge's meadow, and Tallmadges meadow north and west, and with the Indians land east The said tract of land to have, to hold, occupy, possess and enjoy with the appurtenances thereof unto the said John Morris, John Sackett and Thomas Tallmadge, their heirs, executors, administrators or assigns, from the day of the date hereof (September 14th, 1695) unto the three and twentieth day of October Anno Domini, one thousand seven hundred thirty and nine, being forty four years and about five weeks complete, yielding and paying therefore in lien of all rents unto the said George or his order the full and just sum of twelve pounds in current pay with the merchant, part whereof is to be paid upon the signing hereof and the remainder upon the approbation of the General Court, and the said John Morris, Thomas Tallmadge, and John Sackett to make and maintain all the fence for their own security and for the security of the Indians that shall plant there within that field during the whole term of time above written But if the said George or any other of the Indians shall see cause to let any part of that land which is reserved for the Indians to plant, the said George doth bind himself and his successors to oblige them that shall hire to fence their equal proportion by acre as the above said John Morris, Thomas Tallmadge and John Sackett are obliged To the true and faithful performance of the premises the parties above named do engage themselves their heirs and successors, and in witness whereof unto these presents indentured interchangeably set their hand or mark the day and year first above written

Signed, sealed and delivered
in presence of
James Butler,
Danll Dodd

Nayhanatt alias George
his X mark
Rum Tom
his X mark
Ombuyschoe
his X mark

This agreement above written with this proviso of the allowance of the General Court is confirmed,
Before me
Wm Jones, Dp Govr *

May 14th 1696 this deed is allowed by the General Court
Attest Eliazer Kimberley,
Secretary

"At a Town Meeting held in New Haven Feb 24th, 1695, Eleazar Morris prouponded that he might have liberty of ye town to buy a highway of ye Indians unto a small piece of land if he can procure liberty of ye General Court Voted Granted

P 1 Acts and Laws passed by the General Court Assembly of His Maj English Colony of Connecticut Enacted October 1702 †
P 95
An act for well ordering and Governing the Indians in this Colony and securing their interest and lands therein —

* Previous to this *March 4th, 1686*, Deacon John Chidsey, John Potter and John Austin were permitted by New Haven to buy for 6 shillings one quarter of an acre of the *Indians* at the Ferry to build stables for their horses when they went to New Haven The deed was signed by Narranshanott, George Sagamour, Weang and Kehow This place was called Stable Point

† Title page lost

Whereas the bringing the Indians in this land to the knowledge and obedience of the only true God and saviour of mankind and the Christian Faith, as well as a civil and peaceable behavior was one great end Pro fessed by the First Settlers of this Colony in obtaining the Royal Charter, which profession this Court being always desirous in the best manner to pursue—Therefore

P 96 Be it enacted by the Governor, Council and Representatives in General Court Assembled and by the Authority of the same, that the authority and select-men of each town wherein there are Indians living or residing shall take care and they are hereby directed to endeavour to assemble and convene such Indians annually and acquaint them with the Laws of the Government made for punishing such immoralities as they may be guilty of and make them sensable that they are not exemped from the penalty of such Laws any more than His Majestys other subjects in the Colonies are, and for as much a drunkeness and idleness may be looked upon as a great meanes of holding them in ignorance of and predjudice against the Truth of Religion Therefore be it further enacted by the authority aforesaid that no person or persons whatsoever shall directly or indirectly Sell Truck Barter Give or Deliver to any Indian any strong beer ale cyder perry wine rum brandy or other strong or Spiritunus Liquors &c &c on pains of forfeiting the Sum of ten shillings for every pint and proportionable for any greater or less quantity so sold truckle barter given or delivered to any Indian directly or indirectly as aforesaid upon conviction thereot before any Court Assistant or Justice of the Peace proper to try the same One half of which penalties shall be to him or them whether English or Indian who shall inform or prosecute to effect, and the other half when the case is tried before a single Minister of Justice to the Town Treasury, but when tried before the County Court, then to the County Treasury of that County wherein such person shall be convicted —And all Grand-Jury-Men shall take diligent care to make enquiry after and present all breaches of this Act—And the testimony of one witness with other strong Circumstances of the Accusition of an Indian shall be accepted as evidence sufficient to Convict a person of the breach of this Act Provided Nevertheless, that nothing in this act shall be construed to hinder or restrain any act of Charity for releaving any Indian in case of sickness or necessity —And every Indian convicted of drunkeness in this Colony shall forfeit and pay the sum of Five Shillings, or else be openly whipped on the naked body, not exceeding ten stripes for one offence as the Assistant or Justice before whom such conviction is shall in his discretion determine —And if any Indian or Indians shall labor or play on the Sabbath or Lords day within the limits of any town in this Colony and be therefore duly convicted, every such Indian shall forfit the sum of three shillings, or else set in the Stocks one hour, at the discression of the Authorities

P 97 And be it further enacted by the Authorities aforesaid that if any Indian or Indians within this Colony shall wilfully and violently fall upon any other Indian or Indians (except is he such as they are at war with) and murder him or them and be therefore legally convicted, every such murtherer shall be put to death And if the Indians shall not do Just Execution upon such murtherer or murtherers speedily, the next Assistant or Justice of the Peace shall forthwith cause him or them to be apprehended and committed to the Common Goal without bail or mainprize there to remain for a Trial at the next Superior Court, who are hereby impowred to hear and determine the Cause according to Law of this Colony —and whereas many Indians in this government put out their children to the English to be brought up by them and many times the persons having such children neglect to teach them and instruct them in the principles of the Christian faith—Therefore Be it farther enacted by the Authority aforesaid, That every person in this Colony that hath, or shall hereafter take any Indian children of this or the neighboring governments into the care of their families, are hereby ordered to use their utmost endeavors to Teach them to Read English, and also to instruct them in the principals of the Christian Faith by Catechising them together with our proper method —And the Select-Men and Grand Jurors in the respective towns shall make diligent enquiry whether the Indian Children that are or may be put out, as aforesaid, are by their masters or mistresses that have the care of them instructed and taught as abovesaid And if on enquiry said Officers shall find that any such master or mistress hath neglected their duty herein after due warning given, such officers or any two of them shall inform the next Assistant or Justice of the Peace thereof who thereupon shall summons such master or mistress so informed against to appear before him to answer thereto, and if upon examination it shall appear that such master or mistress hath neglected to teach and instruct any such Indian Child or Children put to them, as aforesaid, they shall be fined at the discression of said Authority, not exceeding the sum of thirty shilling, to be to the use of the schools in the Town or Society where the offender lives, and for every three months neglect after that shall suffer the same penalty as often as they shall be convinced thereof, for the use aforesaid —And to prevent Fraud in getting Indians or their children bound out in service to the English—It is further enacted by the Authority aforesaid, that no Indenture made by an Indian shall be accounted good in the law, except to be acknowledged before authority, and be it further enacted by the Authority aforesaid, that no person shall be allowed or admitted to prosecute or recover before any Court Assistant or Justice of the Peace any action of Debt or Detinue or of the case for any goods sold lent or trusted out to any Indian or Indians whatsoever—P 98 And every gun lent as aforesaid to any Indian or Indians shall be forfited one half to him that shall inform and prosecute to effect, and the other half to the County treasury where such prosecution shall be—Provided—Nothing in this act shall be understood to debar any person from the benefit of the law for the recovery of any rent due to him from any Indian or Indians for land by him or them hired or improved—and be it further enacted by the Authority aforesaid, that no person or persons in this Colony whether Inhabitants or others, shall buy hire or receive a gift or mortgage of any parcel of land or lands of any Indian or Indians for the future—except he or they do buy or receive the same for the use of the Colony, or for some plantation or village or with the allowance of the general Court of this Colony—and if any person or persons shall purchase or receive lands of any Indian or Indians contrary to the intent of this Act, the person or persons so offending shall forfit to the public Treasury of this Colony the treble value of the lands so purchased or received, and no interest or Estate in any land in this County shall accrue to any such person or persons by force or virtue of such illegal bargain, purchase or recept

The above paragraph on the revival of the laws was enacted in October one thousand seven hundred and two, to be in force from the first day of December then next in following 1702 And on consideration of the Indians being ignorant of the English Laws and Customs about lands

It is further enacted by the Authority aforesaid that when and so often as any suit shall be brought by any Indian or Indians for the recovery of any land reserved by the Indians for themselves or sequestered for the Use and benefit of the Indians by Order of the Assembly or by any town agreeable to the laws of this Colony, that the defendant or tenant shall not be admitted to plead in his defence his possession or any way take benefit of the law entitled An Act for the Quieting Men s Estates and avoiding Suits Made May Eight, One Thousand Six Hundred and Eighty Four 1684 And to prevent damage that may come to Indians in their Corn Fields, by creatures belonging to the English Be it enacted by the Authority aforesaid that in each town in this Colony where any Indians have fenced fields, there shall be Fence Viewers and Apprizers by such town chosen and appointed, who shall be sworn to view such Indian Fence and to apprize such damage as may or shall be done in their Corn fields by any Englishmans Cattle, Horses or Swine, and the Judgment or apprizement of such viewers and apprizers shall be observed and duly performed and assessed by the Owners of such Cattle, Horses & Swine to the Indian or Indians dammified And the Indians having such fields are hereby allowed to make pounds within their fields to impound and secure horses, cattle and swine trespassing upon them

On page 40 If any Negroes, Indians, or Mulatto offenders in the nature to defame, slander, to be whipt and sold to defray charges and expenses

And the Indian or Indians impounding any Cattle, Horses or Swine shall forthwith give notice thereof to the Select Men of that town wherein such field is, and to the Select Men of two adjacent towns unless the owner is known, In which case notice shall be given to the Owner, and if the Owner does not redeem his creatures so impounded by paying the damages sustained within twenty four hours after notice to them given of same, or if no Owner appears within three days after notice given to the Select Men of that town wherein such field is, shall make sale of such creature or so many of them as shall answer the damage done by such creatures and pay said damage therewith

There was still some town land unoccupied and sufficient for the settlers' wants until about 1717, when the last town or sequestered lands were all sold, and in order to make all purchases of Indian land valid to date

AT A GENERAL ASSEMBLY HOLDEN AT HARTFORD ON THURSDAY THE NINTH DAY of May A D 1717

An act concerning purchases of Native rights of land This Assembly observing many difficulties and perplexities arrising in the goverment *by reason of many purchases of land made of Indian tribes without the preeceeding allowance or subquent approbation of this assembly* which to remove

It is hereby declared by this assembly and the authority therefore that all lands in this goverment are Holden of the King of Great Britain as the Lord of the Fee and that no title to any land in this colony can acceed of any purchase made of Indians, on pretence of their being native proprietrs thereof without the allowance or approbation of this assembly as foresaid shall be given in evidence of any mans titles not pleadable in any court

And farther it is resolved that (In as much as many such purchases have been made and the persons who have so made them or they who claim under them may think they have hard measure if they may not retain some considerable portion thereof in lieu thereof assigned to them) John Hampton Esq Mr John Hooker, and Capt James Wadsworth shall be a Commission or any two of them by such ways and means as they shall think fit, to enquire into and gain a true understanding of all the claims foresaid, and by the true circumstances of the said claims before the assembly in October next and what they may understand may be to the satisfaction of the Claimants either within the bounds of any town with the consent of the proprietors or elsewhere within the ungranted lands of the Colony Together with the opinion thereon to the end, and the sd assembly may settle the whole affair and proceed to the settlemen of all the undisposed lands of the Colony in such manner as shall then be determined, that all future trouble about the settlemen may be avoided,

In 1716, the Rev John Woodward moved from Norwich and purchased a town lot within the old city limits The next year, April 30th, 1717, he was made a freeman and soon after, at town meeting held April 26th, 1720, he, with other towns men, asked permission to buy land of the Indians on the east side At this time Mr Woodward bought one acre of land for a watering place for his cattle adjoining his farm, which he had purchased some time before of the town Again, by record of March 8th, 1720, it is seen that John Woodward bought seven acres and a half more or less for twelve pounds, of John Sock, Sachem of the Quinnipiack Indians, James Senior, James Junior, and Tom, all of the town of New Haven &c This purchase embraced that part of the Woodward estate on the northwest side of Townsend's Avenue, bounded and described as follows "Southerly by line beginning at a Mere stone by the path or way leading down to the place commonly called the South End, from thence running westerly straight to a stone by the farm or land in the present possession of said Woodward, then said tract of land is butted westerly from said stone on said farm up to the field commonly called the Old Ferry Field, Northerly upon the said Ferry Field to a highway leading into said field, from thence northerly and northeasterly upon said *highway* to the said *path* or way to the aforesaid Mere stone"

The Quinnipiacks being "tribute payers" were not regarded by the Eaton settlers to be the sole owners of the soil, for the title to this section of North America was claimed by England by right of the Cabot discovery and later through its occupation, in accordance with the public law of that time, as known in western Europe, and it was under this title, confirmed by the Earl of Warwick's Charter and the subsequent purchase from the native owners of the soil of their pretended right to Quinnipiack, that the squatter colony of New Haven held title, until the younger Winthrop obtained the scooping Charter of 1664 from Charles II Connecticut, which held the title from this king and the old records say· "As of his Manor of East Greenwich in County Kent by fealty owners in free and Common Soccage, and not by Knight's Service"

It was therefore the undoubted right of the town of New Haven to grant permission at a Proprietors' Committee appointed by the townsmen to sell (as the Indians gradually passed away) their right to the lands we now occupy

About 1720, the town lands having all been allotted or sold, the townsmen whose farms adjoined the Indian lands began to encroach thereon, and in order to protect the Indians in their rights, a Proprietors' Committee was appointed as follows We quote from the Proprietors' Records, Vol I, p 1, 1724–1749

"At a meeting of the proprietors of the undivided lands in New Haven, held by adjournment, April 28th 1724 Voted—That there be a standing committee chosen to give notice of the warning for proprietors' meetings for the future, and that they set up a notification of the time and business thereof in writing in some suitable place in each society in said New Haven ten days before said meeting, and that they cause *the drum to be beat in each society* at least three days before said meeting to give notice thereof"

"The Committee chosen are Captain Samuel Smith, Mr Carrington, Mr Nathaniel Yale, Mr John Mix, Ensign Mansfield, Mr John Hitchcock, and Sergeant Theophilus Munson"

At the next meeting of the Proprietors of New Haven, held Jannary 11th, 1724–5, Captain James Munson was chosen moderator for the meeting and action was taken as follows

"VOTED—That Captain Joseph Whiting, Mr Samuel Bishop, Captain Isaac Dickerman, Sergeant Joseph Mix, Sergeant Theophilus Munson, Mr Nathaniel Yale, and Captain Samuel Smith, or the major part of them, be a committee in behalf of the people to treat and fully agree with our neighbors in East Haven concerning the land commonly called *Indian land*, and upon a just and reasonable agreement in the name of the proprietors of the undivided lands of this township, and to make and *execute a quit claim of the said proprietors right unto the Indian lands* to those of East Haven that have lately made purchase thereof, having due regard that necessary planting lands be reserved for the Indians *

About 50 acres was reserved and Captain Joseph Whiting was appointed to receive the money paid for the Indian lands

Jan 10th, 1725–6

"VOTED also that the Committee make report to the said meeting of their opinion about the disposal of the money that the Indian land on the East side is sold for"

Following is the report of the survey of the Indian lands

New Haven, March 25th, 1725

Then measured for John Morris and others of East Haven, several parcels of Indian land, one piece is off the road which goes through the field toward George Pardee's—E end 19 rods wide—S side 47 rods N end 19 rods—W 5 acres ½ 13 rods From the path in the field easterly S side here 106 rods, E end 43 rods wide N side 100 rods wide, W end

* The Indians living on the east side about this date were John, Tom, Jacob, Nimrod, Deliverance, Mary, Jim, Rusack, Ashlow, Jeffrey, Job, Adam, with squaw, Mary, Tim, son of James, Joanne, wife of James, Charles, last Sachem

42¾ wide, content 27 acres and ½—One parcel to John and Eliezer Morriss, *Indian land, North* N end 57¾ wide, N side next Indian Land 57 rods long—More at the east end of John Morriss to Eliezer Morriss 19 rods in same line—E end 60 rods wide from hence 70 to Eliezer Morriss 19 rods more northeasterly to John Morris 62 rods—John Morris here 21 acres and ¼ and to Eliezer 7 acres and 20 rods—John Thompson's lot at North end 5 rods wide wanting two foot and one half—N side 81 rods long, S side 100 rods long, E end 56 rods ½ wide E side 88 rods and ½ E end 46 rods wide, N side 100 rods long 25 acres and ¼

Thomas Smith E end 42 rods wide—S side 100 rods long—N side 106 rods long W end 40 rods wide, 26 acres one quarter and 23 rods Per me John Thompson, New Haven surveyor

The above is a true record of the surveyor's return December 7th, 1725 Per Samuel Bishop, Clerk

Further the records show

At a meeting of the Proprietors of undivided lands in New Haven held by adjournment on the 3d Monday of February, 1726-7, at one of the clock, afternoon

VOTED—That the *residue* of the Indian land that the Proprietors and towns' Committee hath not already signed quit claims to the purchasers of East Haven for, shall by the said Committee be acquitted to any person who will appear to pay the 20 shillings per acre according to the agreement unless the former purchasers who claim the same shall appear before the end of March next and pay the sums aforesaid

At a meeting of the Proprietors of undivided land held in New Haven by adjournment, on the last Monday of December, 1727, at ten of the clock before noon

VOTED—That the major part of the Committee appointed by the proprietors to sign a quit claim or quit claims to the Indian land on the East side not disposed of be impowered on the Proprietors behalf and at their cost to eject any that are on any parts of said land by a course of law and that a major part of said committee sign quit claims to the remaining part of said land not disposed of in the Proprietors name to any person or persons they shall think fit and agree with the purchasers thereof as they shall think reasonable

On Sept 3, 1728, a committee was appointed to receive the money from sale of Indian lands and to loan on bonds at five per cent until Jan , 1733, when, the town voted that the committee deliver it to Samuel Howell, Town Treasurer, and he be authorized to let at lawful interest on good land-security, and the interest for the support of the town poor Also that the public lots above the Blue Hills be paid for out of the money called "Indian Money"

On Sept 1732, voted at town meeting, the public stock of money called "Indian Money ' for the townsmen interest, may be used if they choose towards building a wharf at Old Ferry Point

On Dec , 1732, it was agreed by the proprietors that a committee be chosen to receive Indian land money from Capt Joseph Whiting and to agree with a committee from East Haven about their part

On Jan , 1734–5, Indian land money was voted to be used for the purpose of ejecting Warham Marther from Indian land

At a town meeting held in New Haven April 27th, 1731, it was voted that those of the committee surviving, respecting the Indian lands, or a major part of them, be a committee to transact in the affairs of the land of the new Indian field hitherto reserved for the Indians, viz

"That they will quit the town's claim to said land to John Morris on conditions that he secure to the Proprietors for the use of the Indians 50 acres of land in the town of Waterbury, and oblige himself to said committee to secure the said Indian Field land for the Indian use in the summer as the said committee shall think best for the Proprietors of said town and for the said Indians"

The following verbatim copy from New Haven Land Records, Vol VII, p 342–43, will here come in place, and show the joint action taken by the town and proprietors regarding the sale of a portion of these lands, and gives an illustration of how the other sales, of which there were many, were effected

"To all People, greeting —Whereas the Proprietors and Town of New Haven, by their Committee, having remised and quitted claim unto John Morriss and others the right of purchase and all other rights to the said proprietors and town aforesaid, belonging in those Lands commonly called the *Indian Lands*, lying on the east side of the harbour, in said New Haven, as may appear by deeds of the same duly executed under the seals of Messrs Samuel Bishop and others, Committee, as aforesaid, dated December 7th, 1725, and Recorded, whereby the said John Morriss hath lawful right to purchase the Indian right to the lands acquitted as aforesaid Now, know ye, that we, John, alias George Indian son and heir to George, late Sachem of New Haven, and James and Tom, Indians, sons of James, Indians deceased, and Nimrod, Indian, and Jacob Indian, *being all the men of our tribe* [1727] belonging to New Haven aforesaid, for and in consideration of the sum of twenty and two pounds, to us in hand, before the ensealing hereof, well and truly paid by John Morris of said New Haven, in the County of New Haven and Colony of Connecticut, the receipt whereof we hereby acknowledge and ourselves therewith entirely satisfied, and of every part thereof, do acquit, exonerate and discharge the said John Morris, his heirs executors and administrators, forever by these presents, have given granted, bargained, sold, aliened, conveyed and confirmed and by these presents do fully, freely and absolutely give, grant bargain, sell alien, convey and confirm unto him the said John Morris, and unto his heirs and assigns forever, the several pieces of land hereafter in these presents mentioned, that is to say, one piece of land lying in the new Indian Field, so-called, containing three acres, be the same more or less, and is bounded, northerly by land of Samuel Smith of South End, easterly by John Thompson's land, southerly by John Dennison's land, and westerly by the highway, also, one other piece of land lying in the same field, containing eight acres, be the same more or less, being bounded easterly by the same highway, southerly by Town land in said Morriss' occupation, westerly by the line of meadow fence, and northerly by land called the widow Esther Tuttle's land, the northwest corner being a rock in the meadow fence and the northeast corner a heap of stones by said highway, also, one other piece of land in the same field lying on the east side of said highway containing 27 acres and a half more or less and is bounded westerly by said highway, southerly by Thomas Smith's part, so called, in the same Field, easterly by John Howe's land, and northerly by land of John Thompson, in the same Field also one other piece on the east side of highway, containing twenty one acres and three quarters more or less, being bounded westerly by said highway, northerly by the Indian Land fence, as it now stands, easterly by Eliezer Morriss' part of the same field, and south by John Thompson's part of the same Feld, the northeast corner being a rock in the fence, the northwest corner a heap of stones by the gate in the said highway

To have and to hold the said granted and bargained premises, with all the appurtenances, priviliges and commodities, to the same belonging, or in any way appertaining to him, the said John Morris, his heirs, assigns forever, to his and their proper use and benefit forever, avouching that we are lawfully seized of the premises and have right to dispose thereof as aforesaid and will warrant and defend the said John Morris, his heirs and assigns, in the peacable enjoyment thereof forever, by these presents

In witness whereof we have hereunto set our hands and seals

Dated at New Haven April 28, Anno Domini 1727

Signed, Sealed and delivered
in presence of
Jos Whiting,
Joseph Russell,

John alias George Indian,
his mark L S
James Indian, his mark Seal
Tom Indian, his mark Seal
Nimrod, Indian, his mark Seal

Connecticut SS New Haven, April, 28 1727

Then personally appeared John, George James, Tom and Nimrod four of the Indians within mentioned, sealers of the within instruments, and being made well to understand the same, acknowledged the same to be their free and voluntary act and deed

Before me, Joseph Whiting, Assistant.

The above, with that on the foregoing page, is a true record of the original deed, April, 29, 1727 Samuel Bishop, Clerk

These abstracts suffice to show how the transfers of Indian rights were made to the townsmen by the few remaining Indians

As encroachments continued to be made, an adjourned meeting of the proprietors was held the last Monday of December, 1727, at ten of the clock before noon, and Lieutenant Jonathan Alling and Robert Talmadge were chosen as part of the committee for the taking care of encroachments, etc , etc

"VOTED—That a major part of the Committee be appointed by the proprietors to sign a quit claim or quit claims to the Indian lands on the East Side not designed to be empowered on the Proprietors' behalf and at their cost eject any that are on any parts of said land by a course of law and that a major part of the Committee sign quit claims to the remaining part of said land not dispossessed of in the proprietors' names of any person or persons they shall think fit, and agree with the purchasers thereof as they shall think reasonable "

At a before mentioned meeting of the proprietors, held, viz January 11th, 1724–5, it was also voted—

"That the said Committee make a report to the said meeting of their opinion about the disposal of the money that the Indian Land on the East side was sold for "

and at a town meeting held April 27, 1725, the committee submitted the following to the townmen

"Whereas, we have in some measure agreed with ye Committee appointed by the Proprietors of the Town about buying those right in the Indian lands , and

Whereas, some of the town pretend to some privileges of timber and stone in said land, we judge ourselves not wholly secure from disturbance without consent of the Town, and do therefore desire the Town to empower said Committee to confirm all their pretended right to us and others that shall purchase, and then we shall judge ourselves safe in buying of it We remain your servants,

Jacob Hemingway,
John Morris,
John Denison,
Joseph Tuttle, Jr

The Town, by their vote, empowered the said Committee according to their said desire "

The above signers were some of the principal buyers of the Indian lands Mr Jacob Hemingway was the first graduate of Yale College and the first minister of the East Haven Society John Denison was one of the South End land holders John Morris was of Morris Point, and a descendant of the original planter, Thomas Morris, who built the fine old mansion now occupied by his descendant, Julius Hotchkiss Morris, Esq

Joseph Tuttle, Senior, and Joseph Tuttle, Jr, father and son, were the largest land holders in town They bought land, separately or together, as circumstances required, as also did John and Peter Woodward, who purchased of the town meadow lands between the harbor and the meadow fence and later of the Indians, absorbing finally about six hundred acres

The ferry farm, on the east of the Indian lands, at Red Rock, had been granted to George Pardee, who had kept the ferry for Francis Brown, and who had also bought a part of Mr Thomas Gregson's farm at Solitary Cove, and in 1673, the South End men and George Pardee paid the Indian sagamore George twelve shillings for a road of one rod wide from the Cove to the country road This road (now Townsend avenue) was probably an Indian trail from the ferry to Solitary Cove but not laid out until years afterward

In the Proprietors' Records, dated 27th December, 1686, there is mention of the old way from the town plot to the ferry This road, "led from the corner of State and Grove street to Neck bridge and through the Neck (Fair Haven West) to continue where it now is and from the ferry on the East side, the way to be continued where it is, four rods wide to Stoney River and the ends of our bounds, Branfordward" This is the country road which led from Red Rock, Quinnipiack Bridge, on the east side, across the field and met the road from Dragon (Fair Haven) to East Haven, just south of Mr Wm B Goodyear's (the old Pardee house), then turned east, north of the Benjamin Pardee house, and ran east of Tuttle or reservoir hill, past the late Mr Roswell Lancraft's to Four Corners, where it met the old ferry (Stable Point) road and also the Indian trail from the ferry at Red Rock that was closed when the road was opened under Tuttle Hill along

Dragon bank to Fair Haven (Grand avenue) bridge, finished in 1793 Also of the same date it is recorded "That it is to be continued where it was, that is, from Old Ferry Point, at a place called the stables, four rods wide; and from the way that leadeth to the Sea at Solitary Cove, lying between the Sea and the Proprietors there, and so to go where it doth over the Little or Morris Neck unto South End Farm"*

In 1692, on motion made by the South End men in reference to the highway to the Indian land, it was voted that Thomas Trowbridge, Sergt Winstone, John Potter and Sergt Cooper, or any three of them, be a committee, to "stake out" and settle the way formerly used, as described by the town's former order, and they were to inform themselves "by such as knew how the way went in times past, or ought to go, and make return to the Town of what they did" Also they were to treat with the Indians "to settle the matter lovingly with them"

The following agreement with the Indian sachem George, and signed by him and another on the part of the Indians, and the town, has properly a place here, as it tells of the original layout through the Indian Reservation, now Townsend Avenue

Agreement, New Haven, 10th June, 1692

Vol I, page 533—Whereas there was a *former agreement* between New Haven Towne and the Indians for a highway through the Indian Field to George Pardee's land, yet for peace sake we the inhabitants of South End, together with George Pardee, have given to George the Sagamour twelve shillings in money for which I the underwritten do ratify and confirm ye same, and do grant ye same highway to be on Record Beginning at ye Dirty Swamp by ye Iron Works path which formerly went through out the Field to George Pardee's field or land, which was Mr Gregson's land, for which money I further engage that there shall be but two pairs of barrs or gates through out my land to George Pardee's which I the aforesaid Sagamour George will make or maintain forever And I do further engage myself, my heirs, to secure the same highway to them, their heirs and assigns, forever, from me, my heirs, assigns, or any from or under me, as witness my hand and seal dated as above

Witness for Town	Witness for Indian	The mark of
John Potter	Umbesec	Indian George
John Cooper,	Hasomaug	(Seal)

* This highway along the shore of Morris Cove, bounded by the sea on the west, about 188 rods of sand beach, was changed above the bank about 1835

The said Indian appeared then before me & acknowledged the same to be his free act and deed

Thomas Trowbridge

Agrees with original being examined and compared this day

By me,

Wm Jones, Recorder

The Quinnipiacks when found by the English seem to have had several camps on each side of the harbor and located on high ground above the meadows, as evidence still extant testifies, viz shell heaps, stone implements of war, chase, and kitchen utensils

One of their camps was at "Wigwam point," or "the Old Field," east of Savin Rock, and about the site of the residence built by the late C S Maltby, Esq , where may have been a trading station, and others were at Oyster Point and Hamilton Park, near the river banks and the Oyster Shell Fields

These localities are on the west side of our harbor, and on the east side, southward from Quinnipiac bridge, are unmistakable signs in proof of Indian occupation along Ferry street ridge (the old Indian village and trail) and extending as far south as the residence of Mr George Hitchcock, also at Stable Point and the water side, east of Tomlinson's bridge, near the stone mansion house of the Forbes family, and on the "Raynham" property in "The Vale" near the electric railroad station *

These camps were all on sunny hillside clearings, surrounded by a thickly wooded country, convenient to springs of fresh water, and near their corn and bean plantations, the cultivation of which was done by the squaws, and were bordering on the harbor and rivers, which afforded an abundant supply of shell and scale fish within easy reach, the former taken from the sand banks and mud flats at low tide, the latter by means of brush wires or traps, the use of which the Indians taught the English who were also taught by the red men the art of spearing eels through the ice while imbedded in the mud, and also how to catch clams with the feet, by means of the treading process, a method still practiced by the local fishermen of today

* The highway from Stable Point and Forbes avenue met at Four Corners the Indian trail from Red Rock Ferry

The most important occupation of the Indians in time of peace was hunting for animals, which was done by means of bows and arrows, spears, clubs, stones and spring poles, with traps, snares and pits for fur animals The skins obtained found ready sale to traders who annually made secret voyages to Long Island Sound for the purpose of supplying the increasing demand of the markets of Western Europe The flesh of the animals, fowls and birds captured was also important for their diet, and the skins not sold were useful for clothing and for covering their wigwams, especially during severe winters, during some of which the frost penetrated the ground to a depth of four feet The wigwams were made capacious enough, if need be, for one or more families, they were constructed of poles, each from ten to fifteen feet long, set in an oblong circle in the ground and drawn together at the top with hickory or grapevine ties, leaving a wicker mouth opening for smoke to escape over the circular stone fire-place in the center, over which was a soapstone cooking pot, a most important acquisition to their kitchen

The celebrated Dutch author, John de Laet, Director of the West India Company of Holland in his description of New Netherland, in the year 1624, writes in his journal as follows "From Fresh River (Connecticut) to another called the River of Rodenberg, it is 24 miles, Westerly North and Easterly South The stream (Quinnipiack river) runs E N E and is about a bow shot wide (at the present site of Quinnipiac bridge), having a depth of three and a half fathoms at high water The tide rises and falls about six feet, a S E by S moon causes high water at its mouth The natives who dwell here are called Quirипpeys They take many beaver, but it is necessary for them to get into the habit of trade, otherwise they are too indolent to hunt beaver" De Laet says the exports from New Netherlands from 1624 to 1635 amounted to 80,182 beaver and 9,847 otter skins, valued at 686,527 guilders, this included Mr Pynchon's frequent shipments from the Connecticut river, and the Connecticut and New Haven records show the value and importance of this traffic and indicate the commodity's standard money value in all commercial transactions It is interesting to note that the name "beaver" is still used in this vicinity, as for instance, Beaver Pond, a name specially prominent just now owing to the agitation of the Beaver Pond section for park purposes, and Beaver Swamp,

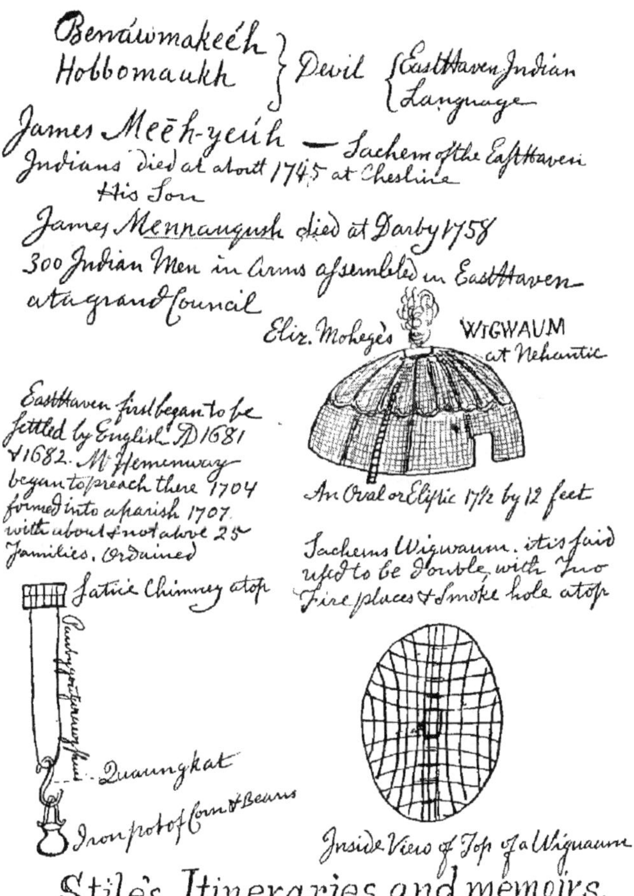

Stile's Itineraries and memoirs. Vol. 1. 1760-62.? pages 496 & 497.

on the Saltonstall estate, which is now being successfully reclaimed.

The covering of the wigwams* consisted of mats of bark or rushes, which were made into mats in the same way that they made their baskets. Similar mats were also used as doors. President Stiles of Yale left several sketches of these wigwams which he made from the originals during the years 1760–70, and gave also a minute description thereof, and I have, with the kind permission of President Dwight and the very courteous attention of Professors VanName and Dexter of Yale University, been enabled to obtain photographs therefrom; and by combining several of these sketches, I have succeeded in producing copies which, no doubt, are fairly accurate, and are surely instructive, giving as they do a fair idea, when compared with other sketches, as to what kind of habitations the Quinnipiack Indians dwelt in at the date of the English arrival.

One sketch made by President Stiles, of George Wawkee's or Oiktee's wigwam, stripped of its mats, and left for the winter, at Niantic, Conn., is no doubt a good representation.

President Stiles has also given us another sketch of Phoebe and Eliza Mohege's wigwam at Nehantic. It was, he says "An oval ellipsis seventeen and one half feet by twelve feet, and is represented as covered with matting, the door open, also, smoke ascending from the top," and he adds a note, saying "Sachems' wigwams, 'tis said used to be double with five fire-places and smoke hole atop."

I am also enabled to quote from the records of the voyage of Verrazano, made in 1524, his description of the round Indian lodges "These lodges were thatched with marsh flags and covered with bark or skins," which corresponds with Pres. Stiles' description of the arbor-shaped wigwams made of poles. Their canoes were 20 feet long and 4 feet wide, and were made without the help of iron. The aid of the fourth element (fire) was called in. They applied fire to the trunk of a tree left standing from which the bark had been taken the year before; the fire being more easily managed on the upright log, and when roughly hollowed out, the tree was burned down

* An Indian house or wigwam was made with small poles like an arbour covered with mats, and then fire in the midst, over which they leave a place for the smoke to go out.'

The natives used in propelling the craft a broad-bladed paddle without a rowlock, as is commonly described in speaking of the Indian mode of rowing

The process of hollowing the tree by fire and rubbing the charred wood with a hard stick or stone frequently dipped in

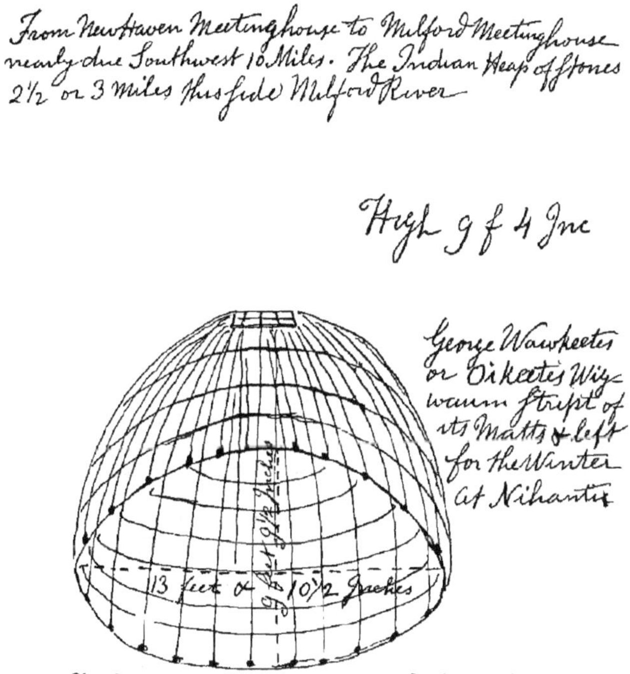

Stile's Itineraries and Memoirs.
Vol I 1760-62? page 4?

water was also applied to shaping the bow and stern, so that in navigating the canoe it might cut the water De Laet mentions the Segains, a more northern tribe than the Quinnipiacs, who made boats of the bark of trees sewed together In these boats they decended the rivers Undoubtedly these were the famous birch bark canoes of the northern Indians

After giving a detailed description of the Nehantic Indian wigwams, which were probably not unlike the Quinnipiacks' in construction and furniture, President Stiles made several valuable sketches of the environs of New Haven These show the sites of the Indian forts, villages, burying places, and of the trails of the Quinnipiacks, also the location of a wigwam in the new Indian field, then (in 1760) occupied by only one Indian and three squaws The location of this solitary habitation is marked on the map of the last thirty acres which were set off to the Quinnipiacks by John Morris in exchange for other Indian land, and which were to him deeded by the Proprietors of the public lands These lands later this tribe sold for 30 pounds, with the permission of the General Assembly, to Timothy Tuttle, through James Adam, who was the last one of the tribe remaining in 1773, and who was then living with the Farmington Indians

In the record of a meeting of the proprietors of the common and undivided land in New Haven, held by adjournment upon the 3d day of January, 1757, is the following entry

"Whereas the Indians living upon the east side of the Harbor had formerly planted land reserved for them, and they being deprived of that privilege, and complaining to this meeting that they were wronged upon that account, this meeting taking that matter into consideration, by vote, do appoint Lieutenant Joseph Mix, Samuel Bishop, Jr , and Roswell Woodward, to be a Committee to search after that business, and examine the matter and see that the Indians have justice done them, and do whatever is needful in order to put the Indians in possession of the land granted them, or do whatever is needful to be done relating to the business of said Indians "

Again we find

"At a meeting of the Proprietors of the Common and undivided land in New Haven, held by adjournment upon the third Monday of December, 1758," it was

"VOTED—That Deacon Mansfield, Caleb Mix, John Mix, Captain (?) Sherman and Samuel Bishop, Jr , be a Committee to search the Records relating to the *Indian Land Money*, so-called and if upon examination of the records, they are of the opinion that the money did rightfully belong to the proprietors, that they report their thoughts unto the next Town meeting, and see what the town will do relating to the money, which money at present lies in the Town Treasury '

Again, at a meeting of the Proprietors of the Common and undivided lands in New Haven held by adjournment on the said 30th day of April 1764, the following action was taken

"Whereas there was an agreement made by John Morris and the Proprietors when the land called Indian Land was sold about 1730 (?) that the Indians should have about *30 acres* of land reserved for their use for planting land, as appears by an instrument under the hand of said Morris, and the Indians are now complaining that they are prevented by the present owners from improving the land according to the original agreement the Proprietors do therefore appoint Daniel Lyman, Esq, Mr Joshua Chandler and Samuel Bishop, Jr, a Committee in the name and behalf of the Proprietors with full power and authority to examine into the state and circumstances of the land and do whatever is needful to be done in order to have justice done the Indians and the original agreement fulfilled" *

The following is from Connecticut Records, Vol 34, p 29:

"To all people to whom these presents shall come Greeting, whereas, the General Assembly of the Colony of Connecticut at their Session in New Haven held by adjournment *January 1769* upon the memorial of Adam, Indian, and the use of the New Haven tribe of Indians, requesting of said Assembly, that the *planting land* reserved for said tribe in the Town of New Haven in ye parish of East Haven which contains about *thirty acres* might be sold and the money received by the sale of such land might be laid out in Farmington for the benefit of said tribe, upon which said Adam was empowered to make sale of the right said Tribe had unto the land aforesaid, which said *Adam soon after died* Whereupon application was made to the General Assembly in May 1770, to empower some other person to convey said land Whereupon said Assembly empowered Samuel Adam an Indian belonging to Farmington, *one of said tribe*, to convey said land with ye same power and authority which was granted unto said Adam, all of which was to be disposed of under the direction of Samuel Bishop and John Strong, all of which appears by ye acts of said Assembly, reference hereunto being had Therefore, know ye, that I the said Samuel Adam, for ye consideration of *thirty (30) pounds lawful* money to be improved for the purposes aforesaid, received to my full satisfaction of Tim Tuttle of New Haven, in the County of New Haven, in said Colony, do for myself and ye rest of said Tribe, by virtue of said act of Assembly, give, grant and convey unto said Tuttle and unto his heirs and assigns forever, all the right, claim and interest challenge and demand, which I and the rest of the Tribe of Indians have in or to the aforesaid land by any means or ways whatsoever, which land was reserved for the use of said Indians and contains about thirty acres and is *fully and particularly described*

* See New Haven Records, Vol IV, pp 528, 561

in an agreement made between John Morris and the Proprietors of New Haven for the benefit of said Tribe which land is fully described in said agreement which is recorded in Said New Haven and is *also described in the acts of said Assembly* relative thereto

To have and to hold the aforesaid land with all the appurtenances thereto appertaining unto said Tuttle his heirs and assign forever, and I the said Samuel Adam do for myself and ye rest of said Tribe by virtue of the power given me as aforesaid covenant with ye said Tuttle his heirs and assigns that I have an absolute right to convey all the right, claim and demand of said tribe of Indians unto said land to him the said Tuttle his heirs and assigns against all claims and demands whatsoever

In witness whereof I have hereunto set my hand and seal June 2nd, 1773

Signed, sealed and delivered
in presence of Samuel Adam (Seal)
James Wadsworth,
Hez Wadsworth

Hartford County Hartford, June 2nd, 1773 Personally appeared Samuel Adam signer and sealer of the foregoing instrument and acknowledged the same to be his free act and deed before me, James Wadsworth, Justice Peace

Hartford, June 2nd, 1773 We the aforesaid Samuel Bishop and John Strong do give our consent and concurrence to ye said Samuel Adam giving the aforesaid deed as witness our hands the date above

Samuel Bishop,
John Strong

Received to Record October 9th, 1773 and recorded by Samuel Bishop, Clerk

Vol 34, page 31

Know all men by these presents, yt I Timothy Tuttle of the Town and County of New Haven in the Colony of Connecticut, for good consideration me hereunto moving especially Ten pounds money received of Joseph Tuttle of said Town, do remise, release and forever Quit Claim unto said Joseph Tuttle and unto his heirs and assigns forever, all my right and interest in Ten acres of land in said Town in the parrish of East Haven which is bounded West on highway South on land of Henry How, North and east on land of said Tuttle, *which is part* of the *planting ground reserved for the Indians* I having *purchased the Indian Title of Samuel Adam* To have and to hold the above remised and released premises with the appurtenances thereof unto him the said Joseph Tuttle, his heirs and assigns to his and their own proper use and behoof, so that neither I ye said Timothy Tuttle nor my heirs nor any other person or persons in mine or their names or in the name, right or stead of any of us or them shall or will by any way or means, have any claim, challenge, or demand upon the premises, or any part or parcel thereof, but thereof and therefrom I and my heirs and all persons claiming any right unto the premises under me or them shall by these presents be forever barred and secluded

In witness whereof I have hereunto set my hand and seal October 9th, 1773

Signed, sealed and delivered
in presence of
Samuel Bishop, Jr, Timothy Tuttle, (Seal)
Jacob Pinto

New Haven, October 9th, 1773

Personally appeared Captain Timothy Tuttle signer and sealer of the above Instrument and acknowledged the same to be his free act and deed

Before me, Samuel Bishop, Jr, Justice of Peace

Received to record October 9th, 1773, by Samuel Bishop, Jr, Clerk

Vol 34, page 28

Know all men by these presents yt I Timothy Tuttle of ye Town and County of New Haven in the Colony of Connecticut for the consideration of a quit claim deed given me by my brother Joseph Tuttle of said Town, of land and meadow which is fully described in said quit claim deed do remise release and forever quit claim unto my said brother Joseph Tuttle and unto his heirs and assigns forever all my right, title, claim, interest and demand yt I have unto certain land and meadow situate in said *Town* in the *parrish of East Haven* one of which pieces of land contains about twenty acres bounded West on highway, South on land of Henry F Hughes, East on Hemingway's land, and North on land of Samuel Tuttle in part and partly on land of Said Joseph Tuttle, brother of said Samuel Tuttle One other piece of land *in the farm where said Joseph Tuttle dwells*, which contains in Quantity thirty two acres and a half and twenty five rods, bounded South on land of Samuel Forbes, West on meadow, East on highway, and North on land I have quitted my claim to, in part which is the next piece described and in part on land which said Joseph hath quitted his claim unto me Also one piece of meadow that contains about two acres, bounded South on Atwater's meadow, West on the Harbor, North on my meadow I bought of Goodsell, and East on my land, and also one other piece of meadow that contains four acres more or less bounded East on Said Joseph Tuttle's land, North on meadow of Samuel Forbes, West on the Harbor and South upon Goodsell's meadow

To have and to hold the above released and claim quitted premises with the appurtenances thereof unto ye said Joseph Tuttle, his heirs and assigns forever, to his and their own proper use and behoof, so yt neither I, the said Timothy Tuttle, nor my heirs nor any other person or persons in mine or their names, or in the name, right or stead of any of us, shall or will by any ways or means, have any claim or demand unto the premises, but by these presents shall be barred and secluded therefrom

In witness whereof I have hereunto set my hand and seal, October 9th, 1773

Signed, sealed and
delivered in presence of
Samuel Bishop, Jr , Timothy Tuttle, (Seal)
Jacob Pinto

New Haven October 9th, 1773

Personally appeared Timothy Tuttle signer and sealer of the foregoing instrument, and acknowledged the same to be his free act and deed

Before me, Samuel Bishop, Justice of Peace

Received to record, October 9th, 1773, and recorded by Samuel Bishop, Clerk

Public Records of Connecticut, 1776–78, Vol I, (Hoadly), Gen Assembly from Oct 10 to Nov 7, 1776, p 41

"Upon the memorial of Hezekial Wadsworth of Farmington praying for the appointment of a Committee vested with the full power to dispose of certain *Indian Right of Land* situated in said Farmington and *Purchased with* the avails of said (sd) East Haven Rights of land so called or at least as much thereof as shall be found to belong to Samuel Adams, an Indian native removed with his family from said Farmington into the Mohawk Country as per mention on file (See copy of Memorial)

Resolved, by the Assembly that Col , John Strong Mr Elnathan Gridley and Mr Timothy Root he and they are hereby appointed as a Committee with full power and authority by sale to dispose of any property or properties of said right of land upon the application of the proprietor or proprietors giving said Commettee satisfaction of his or their determination to leave the State Appropriating the avails of said land to be disposed of to the sole use and benefit of him or them, and in his or their names to Execute a Deed or Deeds to the purchaser or purchasers, and to do every other matter or thing necessary to render the conveyance valid to the law '

From Journal of Town Meetings from December, 1769, to December, 1807

Indian money from sale of lands, how disposed of

At a town meeting held in New Haven by adjournment December 30th, 1774

VOTED That there be the sum of one hundred pounds *or the Indian money* so-called, collected in, and be disposed of to pay for a stock of powder which the Town is obliged to secure by the late act of Assembly, it is also recommended to the several school committees in the Town for *Indian money* so-called, Exchange ye bonds from the Town to the School Committee

Provided they give such security as the said School Committee shall approve of

This last sale of the Indian land was made to Timothy Tuttle, June 2d, 1773, he again sold to his brother, Joseph Tuttle, who in 1796 sold a part of the thirty acres included in this transaction to Isaac and Kneeland Townsend; and they, in

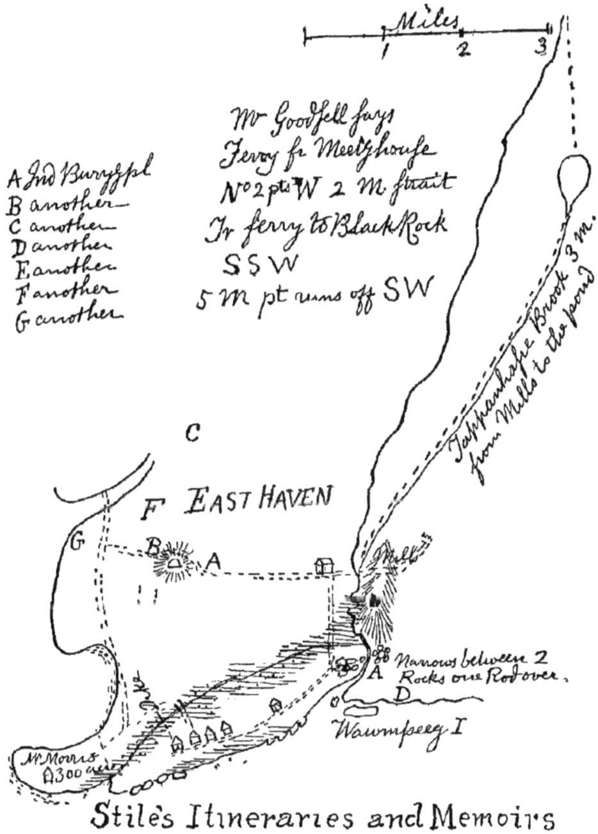

Stile's Itineraries and Memoirs
Vol 1 1760-62? page 403.

1820 sold to William Kneeland Townsend, who dying in 1849, this part of his estate came to the writer, who is directly descendent, maternally, from Joseph Tuttle, father of the aforesaid Joseph and Timothy, who was an early purchaser of the Indian lands, as the records show

In one of these sketches and the first outlying map I have seen of the east side, between the Quinnipiack River and Tapamshasick River (Farm River) is shown the site of seven Indian burying places; also, the island "Waumpleg" (Scotch Cap) at the mouth of the Farm River, and the residence of the Reverends Street and Hemingway near the old meeting-house, the latter located on the northwest corner of the village green The Morris house at Solitary Cove, and five houses at South End were the homes of the early settlers of the Neck, whose money paid for the first bell used in the New Haven meeting-house This bell could be heard under favorable circumstances at a remote distance

These sketches, made in 1760–2, no doubt give us a fairly accurate outline of the "Indian Side" as it was called at this date The sketches have marginal notes, which I have copied verbatim, viz· "James Meeh-yeuh Sachem of the Quinnipiacks or East Haven Indians died 1745 at Cheshire. His son James Mennauquch died at Derby 1758 At one time three hundred Indians assembled in East Haven at a Grand Council Dr Ruggles says There lately died in Guilford (1760) an Indian, the only remaining *man Indian* between Saybrook and New Haven Ferry; there are only a few squaws and children left"

Dodd says "The last Sachem of the Quinnipiacks *Charles* was frozen to death near a spring one mile North of the East Haven Meeting House" He died about 1770

Mr Pardee told President Stiles in 1760, he remembers when the Indians numbered more than the East Haven militia company.

The principal burying place of the Quinnipiack Indians is situated on the land of the Messrs Woodward and a few rods west of the Indian fence, remnants of which, showing its outline, are still extant on the northeast part of Fort Wooster Field, dividing the parsonage lands and How lot from the said field

This place of burial deserves more than casual mention, as it may again prove, as former examinations have, a mine of wealth to those in search of archæological relics

From these graves many relics of the stone age (now in my possession) have been taken, and men now living testify to their having assisted at excavations when many objects of extraordinary interest were exhumed

The late Rev Stephen Dodd, who was for many years minister of the Congregational Society (Stone Church), East Haven, informs us that "the burial place of the Quinnipiack Indians is on the Northeast slope of the Hill on which Fort Wooster stands Some of the graves have been levelled by the Plough but many of them are yet visible" He also says "In the year 1822 I examined three of these graves At a depth of about three feet and one half the sand stone appears in which the bodies were laid without any appearance of a wrapper or inclosure They all lay in the direction of the South West and North-East, the *heads towards* the West Of two of them the arms lay by the side The other had the arms across the body after the manner of the White people The larger bones and teeth were in a sound state The thigh bones of one measured 19 inches in length, the leg bone 18 inches, and the arms from the elbow to the shoulder 13 inches By measuring the sketetons as they lay, this one, it was concluded, was that of a man six feet and a half high"

"No articles of any description appeared with the bones It is said that about fifty years ago some of these graves were opened and a number of Indian implements of war and of kitchen furniture were found in them Few Indians have been buried here within a century past."

Mr Dodd adds "The Indians had a *Fort* on the hill near the burying ground and from that circumstance it was called Fort Hill"

Prof J D Dana of Yale College says "In 1836 he went with Mrs Whelpley's son (of Hillhouse avenue) and opened two graves on Beacon Hill (North-East slope) and took therefrom two skeletons of persons, now to be seen (only the skulls remain) in the Medical College No coffins, or implements for war or chase were found"

The late Dr Levi Ives says While a medical student he and others with him examined the Indian graves of Fort Wooster Hill This occurred about the year 1836 The party consisted of Dr Totten, John Atwater and himself, all medical students They opened thirteen graves from which were taken bones and trinkets One leg bone which had been broken and connected with a ligament, he kept for years as a curiosity, also a skull broken as if by a tomahawk blow These he finally gave Dr Francis Bacon of this city for his collection

In twelve of the graves nothing but bones were exhumed, but in one, which was probably a chief's, a skull with scalp and hair in a good state of preservation was found The hair, which was long, straight and black, had several tailor's thimbles tied in it He also found in this grave a copper pot and glass and pewter vases Mr Wm Woodward ordered the visitors off and forbade their digging up his land, but when told they were Prof. Silliman's students, he allowed them to remain

Mr Horace Day says he went, in 1836, with Prof Dana of Yale College, to examine the Indian graves on Beacon or Fort Wooster Hill They asked permission of the owner, Mr Wm Woodward, who loaned them a spade and shovel They commenced excavating in the northeast corner of the Fort Wooster lot (on the south side of the fence running east and west) in a gravelly soil and dug to the depth of between three and four feet Two skeletons were found sitting with their faces to the rising sun Mr Day carried the bones to his room in College in a large handkerchief, the next morning when he went to look at his Indian nothing remained but a set of teeth The remains were of a middle-aged adult

Mr. Edward C Beecher says "I recall what my grandmother Woodward told me when a child A part of Beacon Hill [Fort Wooster Park] was an Indian burying ground and it was the practice not to bury any of their dead unless some survivor could speak a good word for a dead comrade One of their number died and remained unburied several days because no one could speak a good word for him Finally an old Indian came along and pronounced the dead as being a good smoker then they planted him in a sitting position, facing the east"

The East Haven cemetery was once the site of an ancient Indian fort and according to the records of the village, East Haven, June 13th, 1707, "It was agreed to sequester a piece of land for a burying place on the South side of the *Pond* on

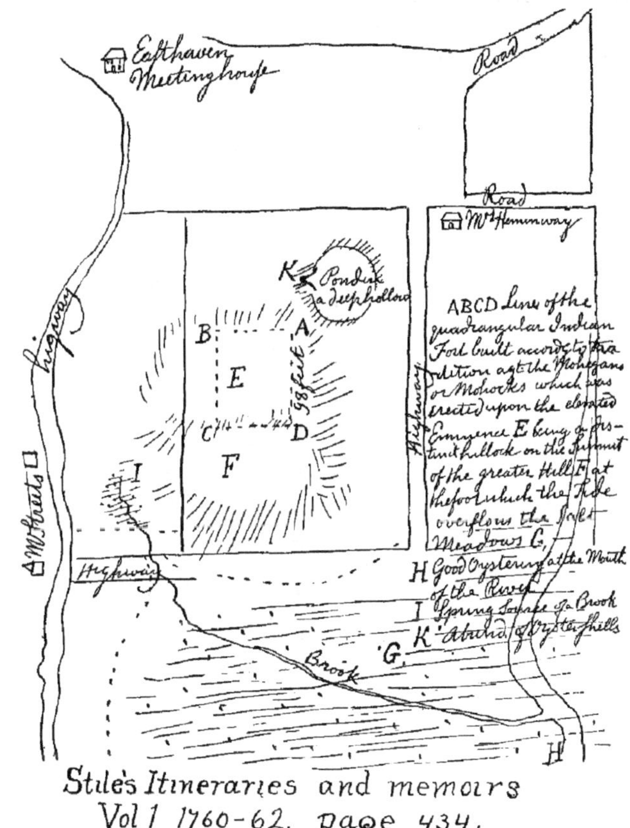

Stile's Itineraries and memoirs Vol 1 1760-62, page 434.

the Fort Hill (*so-called*) as much as may be spared from highways, and watering cattle" This spring and pool existed until the year 1896, when part of it was filled in by the citizens of East Haven in order to beautify the cemetery

This fort, according to traditions mentioned by President Stiles, was defended by the Quinnipiacks against the combined attack from Mohawks and Mohegans Stiles has left a sketch of this fort with East Haven green, old church, Mr Hemingway's and Mr Street's houses, all from an examination made by him on the spot, in company with the Reverend Nicholas Street of East Haven, about the year 1762, and his measurements and remarks I copy verbatim from his diary, Vol I, 1760–2, page 454, and are as follows

Y C Lib Sept 5th, 1892 *Stiles*

ITINERARIES
And
MEMOIRS
Vol I, 1760-62

P 434

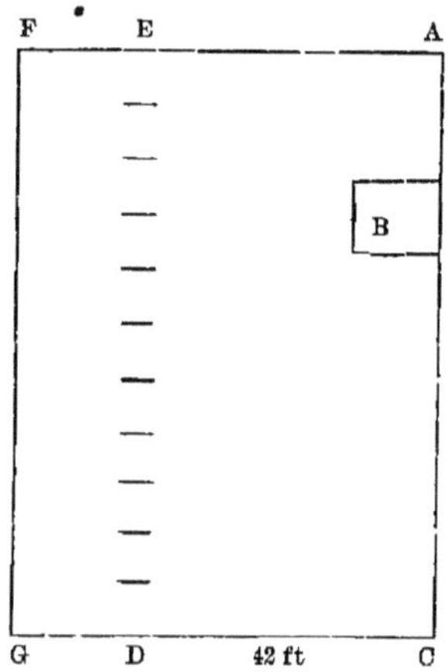

"Indian Fort by Mr Hemingway in East Haven Bury'g yard 42 ft x 86 ft I measured perhaps 30 paces sq

A C The ruins of the ridge of earth very apparent

B Inclosure over the grave of Rev Mr Hemingway and wife on the East side of the old Fort

C D Broken but discernible remains of the South Ridge

A E The North Ridge—this far

D E The line which I measured the length

C D The line of which I measured the breadth I also measured the North side A F and paced from A to C"

President Stiles further remarked. "As we could not determine the West Ridge before we came to the fence which we thought might possibly stand on it, Mr Street who was with me walked from each of these corners A to C about 30 paces each, there we could well discern distinctly the ridge beyond D and E by reason of graves and road; Mr Goodsell afterward told us the West ridge did not extend to the fence and that the whole of the fort would not extend 86 ft which was from 86 ft to 70 ft"

The Rev Jacob Hemingway, whose grave is mentioned, was the first minister of East Haven He was born there in 1683, and died October 7, 1754, aged 71 His ministry there continued for fifty years He said that when he first preached in East Haven, almost immediately after his graduation from Yale College in 1704, there were about 100 fighting Indians in the parish.

In Sir Edmond Andros' time (from March, 1687–8 to 1688–9) the Indians killed in East Haven one Robbins, an Englishman, on the hill between Mr Woodward's and the ferry

President Stiles says. "In 1762 Mr Prout remembers Indians in his time, and hearing his mother say that 100 Indian men were living at a time within her memory There were fifteen or twenty families here in the time of the Cuban expedition in 1740 Many of the Quinnipiacks went off in the Louisburg expedition, 1745, and never returned" Again President Stiles tells us that about 1720 there were between the Ferry (East Side) and Mr Woodward's, twenty wigwams (old Indian village), while in 1760 there was but one wigwam, and this was occupied by a squaw and her son, 16 years old, as already noted This was probably on the last 30 acres sold to Tuttle

This compilation is an abridgment of gleanings from Quinnipiack Indian history and colonial records made during a period of more than forty years' search, with the object to prepare a more extended one for publication later, the detail being too voluminous for condensation in a paper of this kind

In conclusion the writer takes this opportunity to thank the custodians of our public records, the president and librarian of Yale University, and last, but not least, my friend Horace Day, Esq , also Dwight E Bowers, Esq , librarian of the New Haven Colony Historical Society, for their kind assistance in forwarding this compilation for publication

Courier, Sept 6, 1897

INDIANS IN CONNECTICUT —THE CENSUS RETURNS GIVE THE NUMBER OVER TWO HUNDRED

McDonald Furman of Ramsey, Sumter County, S C, writes to the Norwich Record as follows

The following statistics about the Indian population of Connecticut may be entertaining to your readers who are interested in such things, but do not take the time to look them up I get the figures from the admirable compendium of the eleventh census

In 1870 the Indian population of Connecticut was put down as 235, ten years later it was 255, and seven years ago it was 228 In 1870 and 1890, Indians were returned from every county except Tolland, and in 1880 Indians were returned from every county, there were four put down for Tolland county The following was the return of Indians by counties of Connecticut, as given in the census of 1890 Fairfield, 31, Hartford, 17, Litchfield, 13, Middlesex, 5, New Haven, 25, New London, 105, Windham, 32, making a total of 228

It will be noticed that New London county, in the above table, has a larger Indian population than the other counties This was also the case in 1870 and 1880, in the former year New London county had 141 and in the census of 1880 she had 147

While I am on the subject of the Connecticut Indians, I will add that the venerable Eliphalet Fielding (who I suppose is still living) would be an interesting person to an Indianologist for not only is he descended from Sassacus, the great Pequot sachem, but he is also descended from the distinguished Occum family I may also call attention to the fact that it is not fifteen years since Sam Brushell, said to be a descendant of the great Sachem Uncas, was laid to his last resting place in Yantic cemetery

APPENDIX.

SOME

HELPS

FOR THE

INDIANS

SHEWING THEM

How to improve their natural *Reaſon*, To know the *True GOD*, and the true *Chriſtian Religion*.

1. By leading them to ſee the Divine Authority of the *Scriptures*.
2. By the Scriptures the Divine Truths neceſſary to *Eternall Salvation*.

Undertaken

At the Motion, and publiſhed by the Order *of the* COMMISSIONERS *of the* United Colonies.

by *ABRAHAM PEIRSON*.

Examined and approved by *Thomas Stanton* Interpreter-Generall to the United *Colonies* for the *Indian Language*, and by ſome others of the moſt able Interpreters amongſt us.

LONDON,

Printed by *M. Simmons*, 1659.

TITLE PAGE OF THE
QUINNIPIACK INDIANS CATECHISM.

Pierson's British Museum Copy.

Some helps for the
POthſhe Airenamàwetouwúngaſh wutche Eànske-
Indians, ſhewing them how to improve
támbawg; Okkekôod múngai auwaus ten auwá chan
their natural Reaſon to know
nêjek, atumbáuwe penauwuawunk wauhéan webe
the only true God, and
waugh wauwérhummat Mando Jehovah, quah wér-
the true Chriſtian religion. Firſt by
ramâuwe Chriſtianâuwe routâſowank. Negónne ſpe
leading them to ſee the divine Autho-
pummóoawarránau nejek kenâwmen Mandowe tóuh-
rity of the Scriptures
kretáſſowunk wutche God wuskwhéganſh. Néeſee-
Secondly by the Scriptures the divine
terâuwe ſpe God wúskwhéganſh mándowâious wér-
Truths neceſſary to eternall
ramauwúnganſh querâûhikkâmuks re michéme kejá-
Salvation.
hiitawunk.

NAT-

FIRST PAGE OF
QUINNIPIACK INDIANS CATECHISM.

By Abraham Pierson.

QUINNIPIACK INDIANS IMPLEMENTS

Collection of Captain G. E. Landcraft.

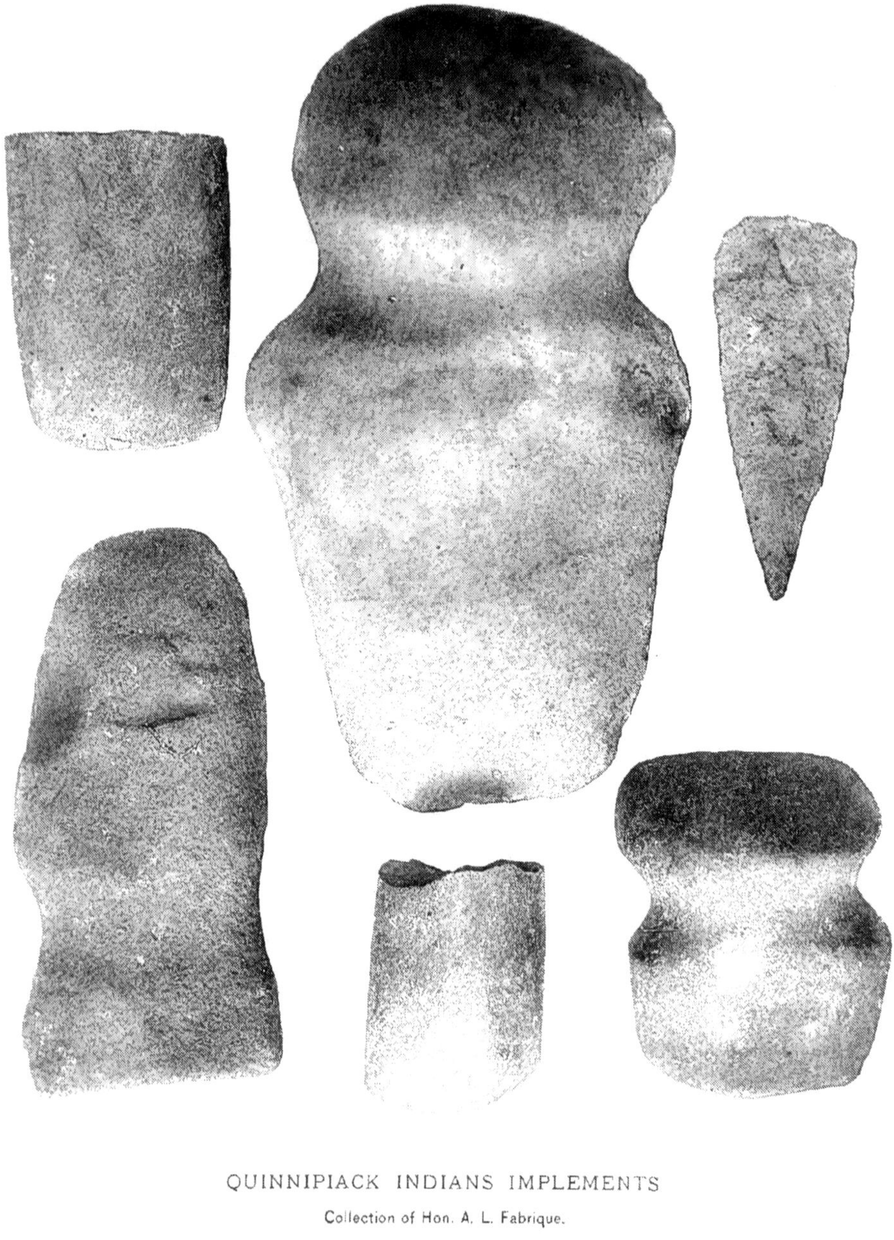

QUINNIPIACK INDIANS IMPLEMENTS

Collection of Hon. A. L. Fabrique.

QUINNIPIACK INDIANS IMPLEMENTS.

Collection of Geo. Hitchcock, Esq.

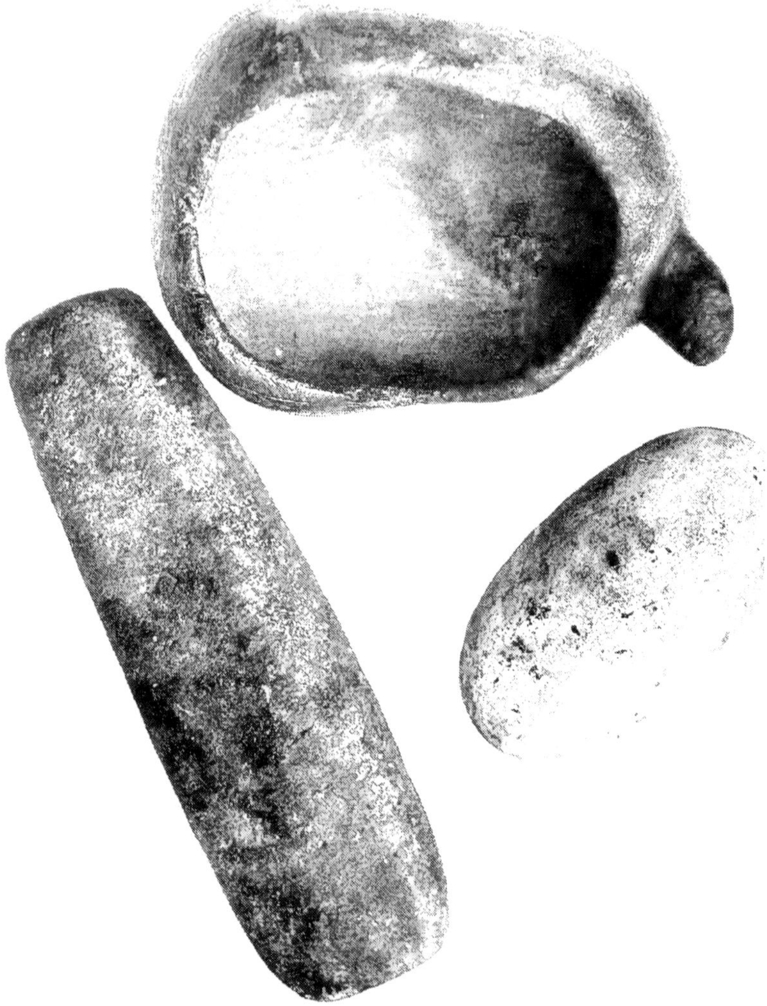

QUINNIPIACK INDIANS IMPLEMENTS.

Collection of Geo. H. Townsend, Esq.

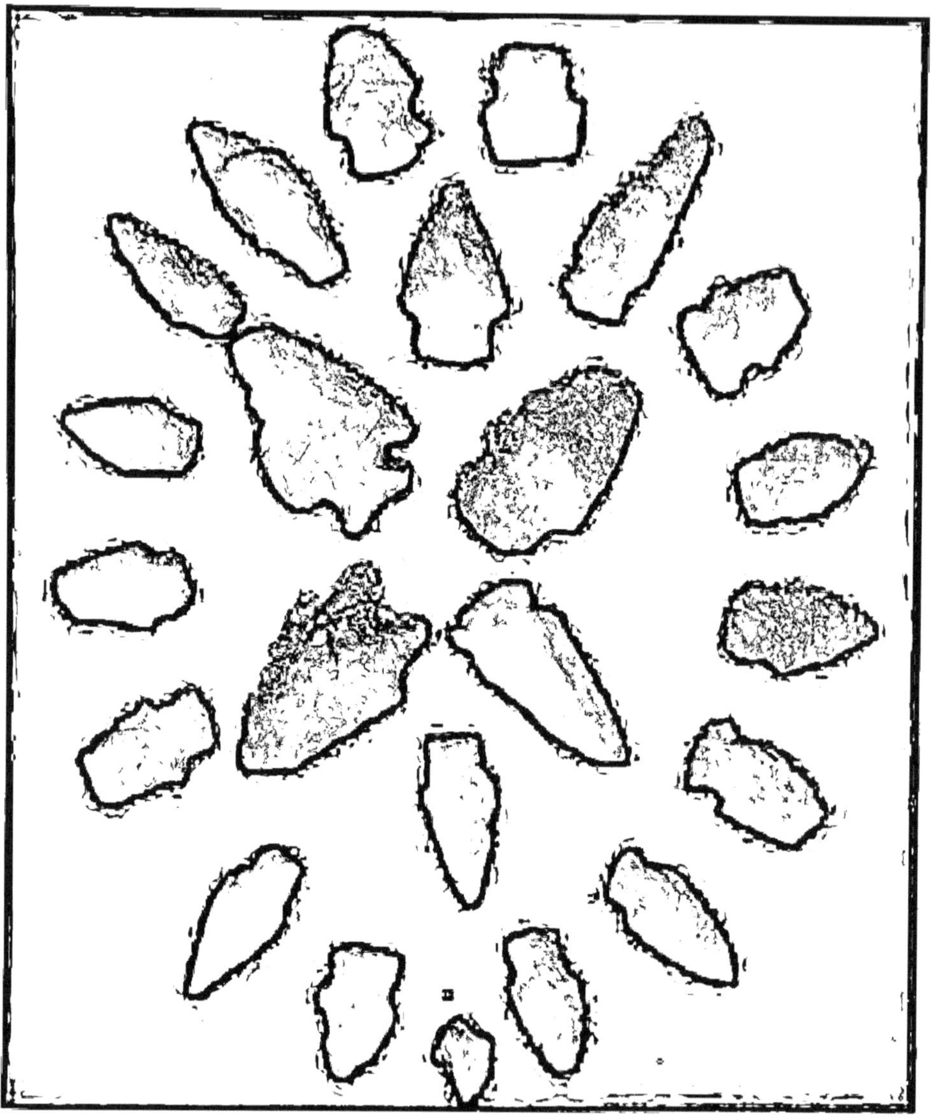

QUINNIPIACK INDIANS IMPLEMENTS

Collection of Chas Hervey Townshend.

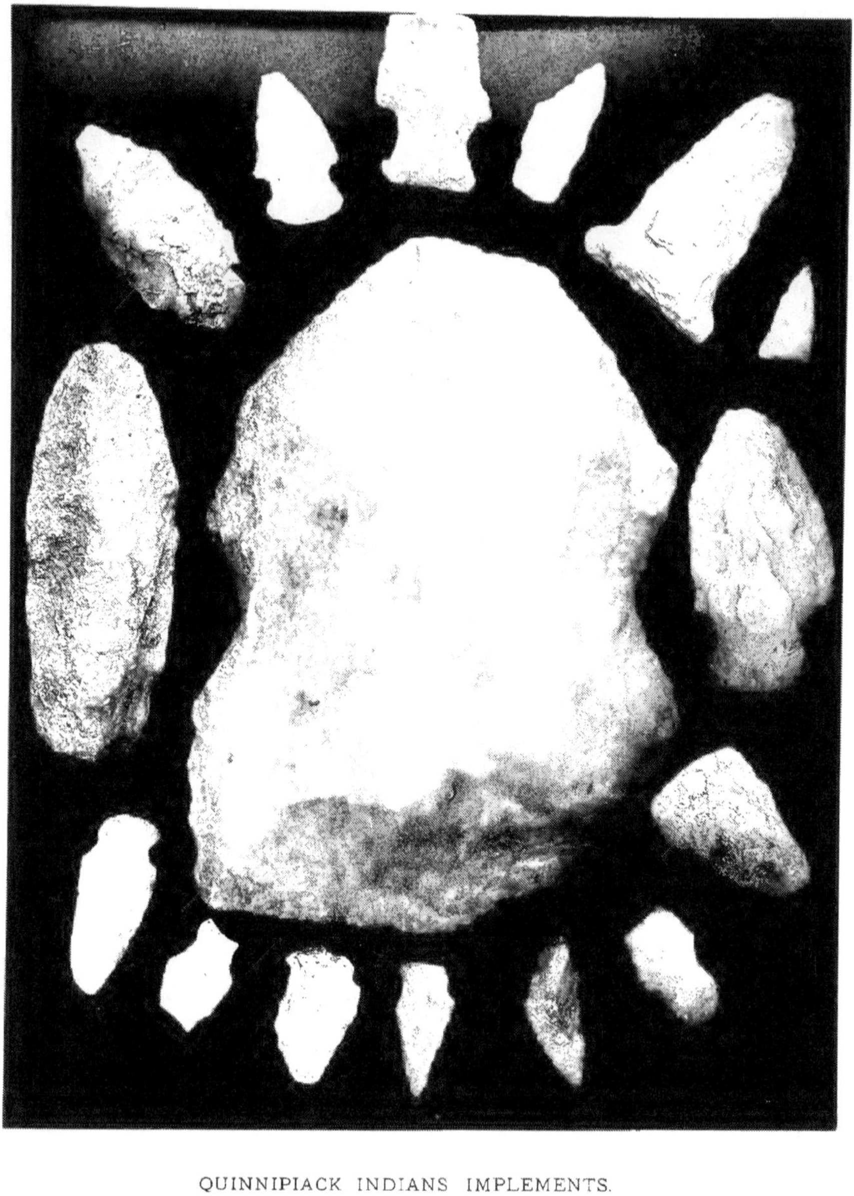

QUINNIPIACK INDIANS IMPLEMENTS.

Collection of Chas. Hervey Townshend.

Facsimile from TOWN RECORDS of New Haven, Conn., of Recorded Treaty between Theopolus Eaton John Davenport and other English Planters, with the QUINNIPIACK INDIANS. Made November 24th, 1638.
Thomas Stanton, Interpreter.

TREATY WITH QUINNIPIACK INDIANS.

Plate 1.

TREATY WITH QUINNIPIACK INDIANS.

Plate 2.

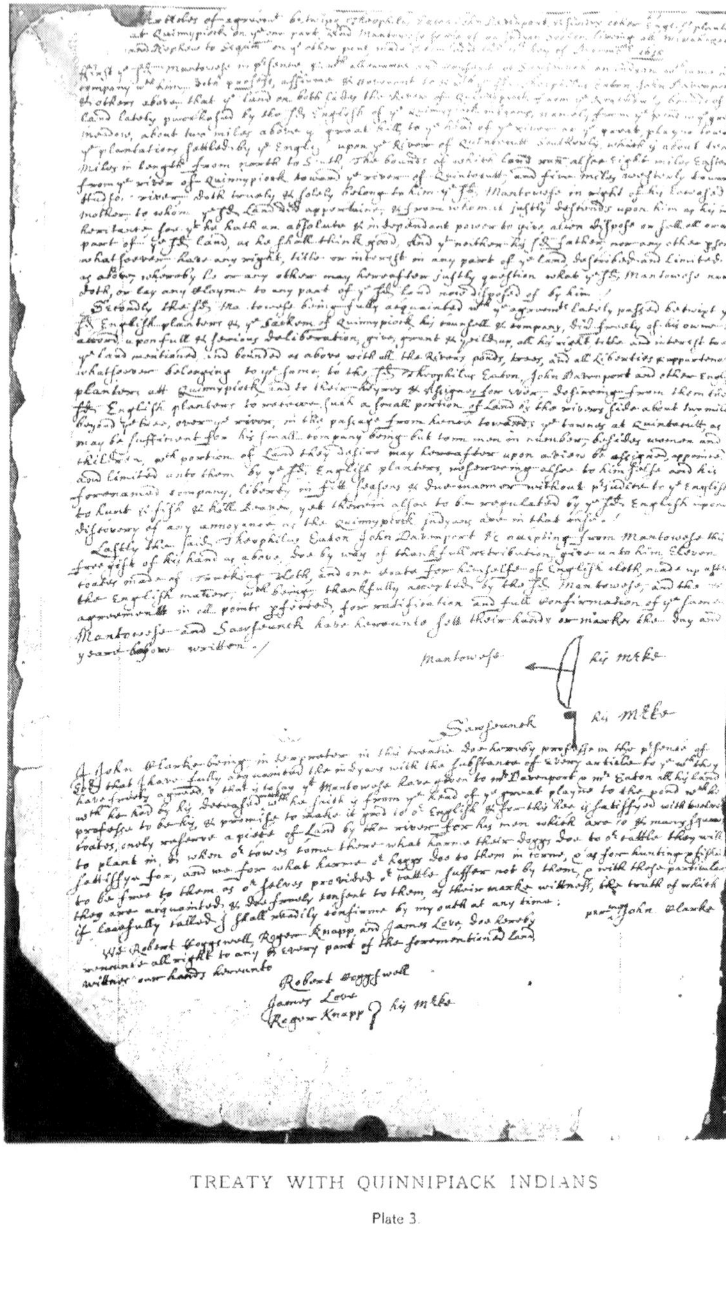

TREATY WITH QUINNIPIACK INDIANS

Plate 3.

CPSIA information can be obtained
at www.ICGtesting.com
Printed in the USA
BVHW040336200419
546083BV00006B/216/P

9 781376 047493